Christmas
with Southern Living
Cookbook

❧❦❧

Make this the best Christmas ever with over
200 of our very favorite recipes from
15 years of *Christmas with Southern Living*.

Christmas
with Southern Living
Cookbook

$\mathcal{T}$his handsome new cookbook will escort you through the holidays with over 200 no-fuss, no-fail recipes. Whether it's scrumptious entrées, dazzling desserts, or fantastic food gifts, we have what you're looking for. Every recipe has been kitchen-tested and proven to promise a merry celebration for one and all.

Oxmoor
House®

©1997 by Oxmoor House, Inc.
Book Division of Southern Progress Corporation
P.O. Box 2463, Birmingham, Alabama 35201

Southern Living® is a federally registered trademark of Southern Living, Inc.

Library of Congress Catalog Card Number: 96-72550
ISBN: 0-8487-1634-5
Manufactured in the United States of America
First Printing 1997

Editor-in-Chief: Nancy Fitzpatrick Wyatt
Senior Foods Editor: Susan Carlisle Payne
Senior Editor, Editorial Services: Olivia Kindig Wells
Art Director: James Boone

page 80

Christmas with Southern Living® *Cookbook*

Editor: Janice Krahn Hanby
Copy Editor: Donna Baldone
Associate Art Director: Cynthia R. Cooper
Designer: Clare T. Minges
Editorial Assistants: Stacey Geary, Catherine S. Ritter
Indexer: Mary Ann Laurens
Senior Photographer: Jim Bathie
Senior Photo Stylist: Kay E. Clarke
Additional Photography/Styling: Cindy Manning Barr, Tina Cornett, Colleen Duffley, Bob Gager, Lisa Gant, Brit Huckabay, Randy Mayor, Howard L. Puckett, Beverly Morrow Perrine, Leslie Byars Simpson, Charles E. Walton, IV
Publishing Systems Administrator: Rick Tucker
Production and Distribution Director: Phillip Lee
Associate Production Manager: Theresa L. Beste
Production Assistant: Faye Porter Bonner

page 11

WE'RE HERE FOR YOU!

We at Oxmoor House are dedicated to serving you with reliable information that expands your imagination and enriches your life. We welcome your comments and suggestions. Please write us at:

Oxmoor House, Inc.
Editor, *Christmas with Southern Living*® Cookbook
2100 Lakeshore Drive
Birmingham, Alabama 35209

To order additional publications, call 1-205-877-6560.

Cover: Turtle Cheesecake (page 74)
Back cover: Herb-Roasted Turkey with Glazed Carrots (page 8), Candied Brandied Cranberries (page 16), Brussels Sprouts with Pecans (page 14), Sausage Dressing (page 12)
Page 2: Herb-Roasted Turkey with Glazed Carrots (page 8)

We Want Your
FAVORITE RECIPES

Southern Living cooks are the best cooks of all, and we want your secrets! Please send your favorite original recipes for main dishes, desserts, and everything in between, along with any hands-on tips and a sentence about why you like each recipe. We can't guarantee we'll print them in a cookbook, but if we do, we'll send you $10 and a free copy of the cookbook. Send each recipe on a separate page with your name, address, and daytime phone number to:

Oxmoor House, Inc.
Cookbook Recipes
2100 Lakeshore Drive
Birmingham, AL 35209

page 16

page 130

page 142

Contents

Herb-Roasted Turkey with
Glazed Carrots (page 8),
Candied Brandied
Cranberries (page 16),
Brussels Sprouts with
Pecans (page 14),
Sausage Dressing
(page 12)

Magical Moments

Entrées and Side Dishes

*P*olish the silver, set the table with your best china, and light the candles—it's time to celebrate Christmas. Create extra special meals with our entrées and side dishes that sparkle with seasonal spirit. Choose from three exceptional entrées, and then mix-and-match your choice with our sure-to-please side dishes.

Herb-Roasted Turkey with Glazed Carrots

1 (10-pound) turkey
Salt and pepper
2 large bunches fresh sage or parsley
¼ cup butter or margarine, melted and
    divided
1 pound carrots, scraped
1 (10-ounce) jar red currant jelly
¼ cup butter or margarine
1 teaspoon coarsely ground pepper
Garnish: fresh sage leaves or parsley sprigs

Remove giblets and neck, and rinse turkey thoroughly with cold water; pat dry. Sprinkle cavity with salt and pepper. Insert 2 bunches fresh sage into body and neck cavities of turkey; tie ends of legs together with string. Lift wingtips up and over back, and tuck under bird.

Line a roasting pan with heavy-duty aluminum foil; lightly grease foil. Place turkey in prepared pan, breast side up. Brush entire bird with 2 tablespoons melted butter; sprinkle generously with salt and pepper. Insert meat thermometer into meaty portion of thigh, making sure it does not touch bone. Bake, uncovered, at 325° for 1½ hours, basting with remaining 2 tablespoons melted butter after 45 minutes.

Cut carrots crosswise into 3-inch pieces. Cut larger pieces in half lengthwise; set aside.

Combine jelly, ¼ cup butter, and 1 teaspoon coarsely ground pepper in a saucepan. Cook over medium heat, stirring constantly, until jelly and butter melt. Brush about one-third of jelly glaze over turkey. Arrange carrot around turkey in pan, and brush lightly with jelly glaze.

Bake, uncovered, 2½ additional hours or until thermometer registers 180°, brushing carrot and turkey with remaining glaze every 15 minutes. (If turkey starts to brown too much, cover loosely with foil to prevent excessive browning, if necessary.) Let turkey stand 15 minutes before carving.

Transfer turkey and carrot to a serving platter, reserving liquid in pan; skim and discard fat from liquid. Place liquid in a medium saucepan; bring to a boil. Cook, uncovered, 8 minutes or until slightly thickened and reduced by one-third. Brush turkey with about ⅓ cup reduced liquid. Pour remaining liquid over carrot. Garnish, if desired. **Yield:** 10 servings.

Orange-Glazed Ham

Pair this citrusy ham with sassy Asparagus with Jalapeño Hollandaise Sauce (page 13) and Roasted Potato Medley (page 15). Generous slices of Special Chocolate Cake (page 64) will end things on a sweet note.

1 (7- to 8-pound) smoked, fully cooked
     ham half
1 cup orange juice
1 cup ginger ale
½ cup firmly packed brown sugar
2 tablespoons vegetable oil
1 tablespoon white vinegar
2 teaspoons dry mustard
½ teaspoon ground ginger
¼ teaspoon ground cloves
Garnishes: fresh parsley sprigs, orange slices,
     candied crabapples

Remove skin from ham; if necessary, trim fat to ¼- to ⅛-inch thickness. Place ham in a large heavy-duty, zip-top plastic bag. Combine orange juice and next 7 ingredients; pour marinade over ham. Seal bag, and place in a shallow pan or dish; chill 8 hours, turning occasionally.

Remove ham from marinade, reserving 1 cup marinade; discard remaining marinade. Place ham, fat side up, on a rack in a shallow roasting pan; insert meat thermometer, making sure it does not touch fat or bone. Bake, uncovered, at 325° for 2 to 2½ hours or until meat thermometer registers 140°, basting with reserved marinade every 20 minutes. (If ham starts to brown too much, cover loosely with aluminum foil after 1 hour to prevent excessive browning, if necessary.) Place ham on a serving platter. Garnish, if desired. **Yield:** 14 servings.

NOTE: Leftover ham will keep in the refrigerator 4 to 5 days. Break free from the post-holiday sandwich routine, and use the ham in omelets, pasta salads, or pot pies.

Orange-Glazed Ham

Beef Tenderloin with Champagne-Mustard Sauce

A bubbly burst of champagne adds festive flair to the cream sauce escorting this beef tenderloin.

½ cup red wine vinegar
¼ cup vegetable oil
½ teaspoon salt
½ teaspoon pepper
½ teaspoon dried thyme
1 (5- to 6-pound) beef tenderloin, trimmed
Garnishes: fresh thyme sprigs, shallots
Champagne-Mustard Sauce

Beef Tenderloin with Champagne-Mustard Sauce

Combine first 5 ingredients. Place tenderloin in a large shallow dish; pour marinade over tenderloin. Cover and chill 8 hours, turning tenderloin occasionally.

Remove tenderloin from marinade, reserving marinade. Bring marinade to a boil; remove from heat. Place tenderloin on a rack in a roasting pan. Bake at 425° for 1 hour or until a meat thermometer inserted in thickest portion registers 145° (medium-rare) to 160° (medium), basting occasionally with marinade. Slice tenderloin. Garnish, if desired. Serve with Champagne-Mustard Sauce. **Yield:** 8 servings.

Champagne-Mustard Sauce
1 tablespoon minced shallot
1 tablespoon vegetable oil
½ cup champagne
2 tablespoons butter or margarine
2 tablespoons all-purpose flour
1 cup half-and-half
2 tablespoons butter or margarine, softened
1 tablespoon Dijon mustard

Cook shallot in hot oil in a small skillet over medium-high heat, stirring constantly, until tender; add champagne. Bring to a boil, and boil until mixture is reduced to ¼ cup. Pour champagne mixture through a wire-mesh strainer into a small bowl, discarding shallot; set champagne mixture aside.

Melt 2 tablespoons butter in a heavy saucepan over low heat; add flour, stirring until smooth. Cook 1 minute, stirring constantly. Gradually add half-and-half; cook over medium heat, stirring constantly, until mixture is thickened and bubbly. Add reduced champagne mixture, butter, and mustard, stirring until butter melts; cool slightly. **Yield:** 1⅓ cups.

Oyster-Artichoke Soup

Tender curly morsels of oysters mingle with chunks of artichoke hearts in this velvety cream soup. Snippets of fresh green onions and parsley subtly season the combo.

2 (12-ounce) containers fresh Standard
      oysters
½ cup butter or margarine
2 bunches green onions, chopped
6 bay leaves
⅛ teaspoon dried thyme
⅛ teaspoon ground red pepper
¼ cup all-purpose flour
2 (14½-ounce) cans chicken broth
1 (14-ounce) can artichoke hearts, drained
      and cut into eighths
2 teaspoons chopped fresh parsley
1 cup whipping cream

Drain oysters, reserving 1 cup liquid. Cut each oyster into fourths. Set oysters and liquid aside.

Melt butter in a Dutch oven over medium heat. Add green onions and next 3 ingredients; cook, stirring constantly, until green onions are tender. Add flour, stirring until blended. Cook 1 minute, stirring constantly. Gradually stir in reserved oyster liquid and chicken broth. Bring to a boil; reduce heat, and simmer, uncovered, 15 minutes. Remove and discard bay leaves. Add oysters, artichoke hearts, and parsley; simmer, uncovered, 10 minutes. Stir in whipping cream, and cook just until thoroughly heated. Serve immediately. **Yield:** 8 cups.

Fresh Mushroom Soup

½ cup butter or margarine
1½ cups chopped green onions with tops
1 pound fresh mushrooms, sliced
¼ cup plus 2 tablespoons all-purpose flour
¼ teaspoon ground white pepper
3 cups chicken broth
3 cups milk

Melt butter in a Dutch oven; add green onions, and cook, stirring constantly, 3 to 4 minutes or until tender. Add mushrooms, and cook 2 minutes, stirring constantly. Stir in flour and pepper; cook over medium heat 2 minutes, stirring constantly. Gradually add chicken broth and milk, stirring until blended; bring just to a boil over low heat, stirring constantly. **Yield:** 9 cups.

Oyster-Artichoke
Soup

Sausage Dressing (photo on page 6)

Southern sensibilities favor cornbread crumbs when it comes to making dressing. Choose either hot or mild ground pork sausage to create this go-with-everything side dish.

1 pound ground pork sausage
4 stalks celery, diced
2 medium onions, diced
5 cups cornbread crumbs
3 cups white bread cubes, toasted
3½ cups chicken or turkey broth
2 large eggs, lightly beaten
2 teaspoons rubbed sage
¼ teaspoon pepper

Cook first 3 ingredients in a large skillet over medium heat until sausage is browned and vegetables are tender, stirring until sausage crumbles. Drain.

Combine sausage mixture, cornbread crumbs, and remaining ingredients in a large bowl, stirring mixture well.

Spoon mixture into a lightly greased 13- x 9- x 2-inch baking dish.

Bake, uncovered, at 350° for 1 hour or until lightly browned and thoroughly heated. **Yield:** 8 servings.

Noodle-Rice Casserole

French onion soup and pleasantly salty soy sauce flatter this casserole. Brown the pasta in butter to intensify the flavor.

¼ cup butter or margarine
3 ounces angel hair pasta, broken into
      1½-inch pieces
1 cup long-grain rice, uncooked
¾ teaspoon chicken-flavored bouillon
      granules
2 cups water
1 (10½-ounce) can French onion soup,
      undiluted
1 (8-ounce) can sliced water chestnuts,
      drained
1 teaspoon soy sauce

Melt butter in a large skillet over medium heat. Add pasta, and cook, stirring constantly, until golden. Remove from heat.

Stir in rice and remaining ingredients; pour into a lightly greased 8-inch square baking dish. Bake, uncovered, at 350° for 40 to 50 minutes, stirring once. **Yield:** 6 servings.

Southwestern Rice Pilaf

7 cups water
2½ tablespoons chicken-flavored bouillon
      granules
1 tablespoon ground cumin
3 cups long-grain rice, uncooked
3 tablespoons butter or margarine
1 cup pine nuts or slivered almonds
¾ cup chopped green onions

Combine first 3 ingredients in a Dutch oven; bring to a boil, and stir in rice. Cover, reduce heat, and simmer 20 minutes or until liquid is absorbed and rice is tender.

Melt butter in a skillet; add nuts, and cook, stirring constantly, until golden. Stir nuts and green onions into rice. **Yield:** 12 servings.

Asparagus with Jalapeño Hollandaise Sauce

A sprinkling of diced jalapeño pepper and pimiento caps off these hollandaise-enhanced asparagus spears in colorful holiday fashion. To save time and effort, cook two 10-ounce packages of frozen asparagus spears instead of the fresh vegetable.

1½ pounds fresh asparagus or 2 (10-ounce) packages frozen asparagus spears
1 (0.9-ounce) package hollandaise sauce mix*
2 tablespoons grated Parmesan cheese
1 tablespoon seeded and diced jalapeño pepper
2 teaspoons diced pimiento
Garnishes: fresh cilantro sprigs, lemon slices, red jalapeño pepper fan

Snap off tough ends of asparagus. Remove scales with a vegetable peeler, if desired. Arrange asparagus in a steamer basket over boiling water. Cover and steam 8 to 10 minutes or until crisp-tender. Arrange asparagus on a serving plate, and keep warm.

Prepare hollandaise sauce mix according to package directions; stir in Parmesan cheese, diced jalapeño pepper, and pimiento. Serve over asparagus. Garnish, if desired. **Yield:** 6 servings.

NOTE: You can substitute 1½ pounds fresh broccoli or 2 (10-ounce) packages frozen broccoli spears for the asparagus. If using fresh broccoli, remove leaves and cut off tough ends of the stalks; discard. Cut into spears, and steam as directed.

* For hollandaise sauce, we used Knorr brand.

Asparagus with Jalapeño Hollandaise Sauce

Lemony Broccoli

1½ pounds fresh broccoli
¼ cup water
¼ cup butter or margarine, cut into small pieces
3 tablespoons fresh lemon juice
1 teaspoon dried basil
½ teaspoon salt
¼ teaspoon pepper
6 lemon rind rings

Remove and discard broccoli leaves and tough ends of stalks. Cut broccoli into spears. Arrange broccoli in an 11- x 7- x 1½-inch baking dish, stem ends out; add water. Cover tightly with heavy-duty plastic wrap; fold back a small corner of wrap to allow steam to escape. Microwave at HIGH 7 to 8 minutes or just until crisp-tender; drain. Add butter and next 4 ingredients; toss gently. Arrange broccoli spears in lemon rind rings. **Yield:** 6 servings.

Julienned Vegetable
Sauté

Brussels Sprouts with Pecans

(photo on page 6)

2 pounds fresh brussels sprouts
1 cup water
¼ teaspoon salt
½ cup butter or margarine
1 cup coarsely chopped pecans
1 (2-ounce) jar diced pimiento, drained
¼ cup minced fresh parsley
2 tablespoons lemon juice

Wash brussels sprouts thoroughly; remove discolored leaves. Cut off stem ends, and slash bottom of each sprout with a shallow x. Combine brussels sprouts, water, and salt in a large saucepan; bring to a boil over medium-high heat. Cover, reduce heat, and simmer 8 to 10 minutes or until tender. Drain and place in a serving dish; keep warm.

Melt butter in a skillet over medium heat, and add pecans; cook, stirring constantly, until pecans are toasted. Stir in pimiento, parsley, and lemon juice. Pour over brussels sprouts; serve immediately. **Yield:** 12 servings.

NOTE: You can substitute 4 (10-ounce) packages frozen brussels sprouts for 2 pounds fresh. Cook according to package directions.

Julienned Vegetable Sauté

Matchsticks of brightly colored vegetables tumble in reckless abandon amid bits of onion, garlic, and basil.

1 large red bell pepper, cut into very thin
    strips
1 large yellow bell pepper, cut into very thin
    strips
2 large carrots, scraped and cut into very
    thin strips
1 medium onion, chopped
2 cloves garlic, minced
⅓ cup olive oil
2 large zucchini, cut into very thin
    strips
2 teaspoons dried basil
½ teaspoon salt
½ teaspoon pepper
Garnish: fresh basil sprig

Cook first 5 ingredients in hot oil in a large skillet over medium heat, stirring constantly. Add zucchini strips, and cook, stirring constantly, 2 minutes or until vegetables are tender. Stir in basil, salt, and pepper. Garnish, if desired. **Yield:** 8 servings.

Squash and Snow Pea Medley

2 cloves garlic, pressed
¼ cup butter or margarine
2 medium zucchini, cut into very thin strips
    (about ¾ pound)
2 medium-size yellow squash, cut into very
    thin strips (about ¾ pound)
¼ pound fresh snow pea pods or
    ½ (6-ounce) package frozen snow
    pea pods, thawed
½ teaspoon dried oregano

Place garlic and butter in an 11- x 7- x 1½-inch baking dish; microwave at HIGH 1 minute or until butter melts. Add zucchini and remaining ingredients, stirring well. Cover tightly with heavy-duty plastic wrap; fold back a small corner of wrap to allow steam to escape. Microwave at HIGH 5 to 6 additional minutes or until vegetables are crisp-tender, stirring after 3 minutes. **Yield:** 8 servings.

Roasted Potato Medley

Pungent thyme and spicy cracked pepper heighten the sweet, mellow essence of roasted potatoes. Try fresh basil, rosemary, sage, or oregano in place of thyme to give the medley a different perspective.

1½ pounds red potatoes, peeled and cut into
    ½-inch slices
½ pound sweet potatoes, peeled and cut into
    ½-inch slices
3 tablespoons olive oil
1 tablespoon chopped fresh thyme or
    1 teaspoon dried thyme
½ teaspoon salt
½ teaspoon cracked pepper

Place potato in a large heavy-duty, zip-top plastic bag; add oil, and shake gently until coated.

Place potato in a single layer in a lightly greased 15- x 10- x 1-inch jellyroll pan or roasting pan. Bake, uncovered, at 500° on bottom oven rack for 12 minutes on each side or until tender. Sprinkle with thyme, salt, and pepper. Serve immediately. **Yield:** 6 servings.

Sweet Potatoes with Apples

A kiss of honey, a spritz of orange juice, and a golden crown of toasty marshmallows elevate this sweet potato-apple casserole to lofty heights.

6 large sweet potatoes (about 5 pounds)
3 tablespoons frozen orange juice
    concentrate, thawed and undiluted
2 tablespoons water
2 tablespoons honey
1 tablespoon butter or margarine, melted
¼ cup sugar
2 Golden Delicious apples, peeled and thinly
    sliced
20 large marshmallows, halved

Cook sweet potatoes in boiling water to cover 25 minutes or until tender. Drain; cool. Peel sweet potatoes, and place in a large mixing bowl.

Combine orange juice concentrate and next 3 ingredients; stir well. Add ⅓ cup orange juice mixture and sugar to sweet potatoes. Reserve remaining orange juice mixture. Beat sweet potato mixture at medium speed of an electric mixer until smooth.

Spoon mixture into a greased shallow 2½-quart casserole; smooth top. Arrange apple slices over sweet potato mixture; brush apple slices with remaining orange juice mixture. Bake, uncovered, at 350° for 20 minutes. Arrange marshmallow halves over apple slices; bake 20 additional minutes or until marshmallows are puffed and lightly browned. **Yield:** 12 servings.

Double Berry
Salad

Candied Brandied Cranberries

(photo on page 6)

A splash of brandy spikes this sweet and succulent cranberry creation.

3 (12-ounce) packages fresh or frozen
    cranberries, thawed
3 cups sugar
½ cup brandy

    Arrange cranberries evenly in a single layer in two lightly greased 15- x 10- x 1-inch jellyroll pans. Sprinkle sugar evenly over cranberries in each pan. Cover tightly with aluminum foil; bake at 350° for 1 hour, switching pans to opposite oven racks after 30 minutes.

    Spoon cranberry mixture into a large serving bowl; stir in brandy. Let cool. Serve at room temperature or cover and chill. **Yield:** 5½ cups.

NOTE: You can store Candied Brandied Cranberries, covered, in the refrigerator up to 1 week.

Double Berry Salad

Ruby-red raspberries and cranberries blend with royal finesse. You can redefine this berry duo with a double dose of cranberries by substituting a package of cranberry-flavored gelatin in place of the raspberry.

1 (3-ounce) package raspberry-flavored
    gelatin
1 cup boiling water
1 (16-ounce) can whole-berry cranberry
    sauce
¾ cup finely chopped celery
½ cup chopped pecans
Lettuce leaves
Garnish: celery leaves, fresh cranberries

    Combine gelatin and boiling water, stirring 2 minutes or until gelatin dissolves. Chill until mixture is the consistency of unbeaten egg white. Stir in cranberry sauce, celery, and pecans.

    Spoon mixture into lightly oiled individual molds or 4-cup mold. Cover and chill until firm. Unmold onto a lettuce-lined plate. Garnish, if desired. **Yield:** 8 servings.

Gingered Peach Salad

1 (29-ounce) can spiced peaches, undrained
1 (8-ounce) can unsweetened crushed
     pineapple, undrained
1 (3-ounce) package orange-flavored gelatin
1 (3-ounce) package lemon-flavored gelatin
1 cup boiling water
1 tablespoon lemon juice
1 tablespoon orange juice
1 teaspoon ground ginger
½ teaspoon salt
½ cup chopped celery
½ cup chopped pecans
Lettuce leaves
½ cup sour cream
¼ teaspoon ground ginger
Garnish: celery leaves

Drain peaches and crushed pineapple, reserving 1¾ cups liquid; set liquid aside. Chop peaches; set peaches and pineapple aside.

Combine gelatins and boiling water, stirring 2 minutes or until gelatins dissolve. Stir in reserved liquid, lemon juice, and next 3 ingredients. Add reserved fruit, celery, and pecans, stirring well.

Pour into a lightly oiled 9-inch square dish. Cover and chill until firm. Cut into squares. Serve on lettuce leaves. Combine sour cream and ¼ teaspoon ginger; spoon sour cream mixture evenly over each serving. Garnish, if desired. **Yield:** 9 servings.

Company Salad with Raspberry Vinaigrette

Begin creating this company-worthy salad ahead by tearing the greens, toasting the walnuts, and shaking the vinaigrette. Slice the fruit just before serving; then toss everything together. Voilà—an impressive salad for eight.

1 head Bibb lettuce, torn into bite-size
     pieces
½ pound fresh spinach, torn into bite-size
     pieces
2 oranges, peeled and sectioned
2 Red Delicious apples, unpeeled and thinly
     sliced
1 kiwifruit, peeled and thinly sliced
½ cup coarsely chopped walnuts, toasted
Raspberry Vinaigrette

Combine all ingredients except Raspberry Vinaigrette in a large salad bowl. Add vinaigrette, and toss gently to coat. Serve immediately. **Yield:** 8 servings.

Raspberry Vinaigrette
½ cup vegetable or walnut oil
¼ cup raspberry vinegar
1 tablespoon honey
½ teaspoon grated orange rind
¼ teaspoon salt
⅛ teaspoon pepper

Combine all ingredients in a jar; cover tightly, and shake vigorously. Chill vinaigrette thoroughly. **Yield:** ¾ cup.

Pork Tenderloin
Appetizer
Sandwiches
(page 30)

Pesto Dip (page 21)

Merry Munchies

Appetizers

Festive gatherings with family and friends make the holidays a cherished time of year. Get your merry-making off to a superb start with these munchies. Recipes range from elegant to casual. Many can be prepared ahead, so you can make even unexpected guests feel welcomed.

Glorious Amaretto
Cheese Dip

Glorious Amaretto Cheese Dip

1 cup (4 ounces) shredded sharp Cheddar
    cheese
½ (8-ounce) package cream cheese, softened
2 to 3 tablespoons amaretto
1 tablespoon brandy
½ cup finely chopped almonds, toasted
Garnish: finely chopped toasted almonds

Combine all ingredients except almonds in a
mixing bowl; beat at medium speed of an electric
mixer until smooth. Stir in ½ cup almonds.
Spoon into a serving dish. Garnish, if desired.
Serve with fresh fruit or crackers. **Yield:** about
1¼ cups.

Spinach Dip

1 (10-ounce) package frozen chopped
    spinach, thawed and well drained
½ cup sour cream
½ cup mayonnaise or salad dressing
¼ cup chopped green onions
1½ teaspoons lemon juice
½ teaspoon dried dillweed

Combine all ingredients in a bowl; cover and
chill at least 2 hours. Serve with fresh vegetables.
Yield: 2 cups.

Overnight Shrimp Dip

*Fresh lemon juice, Worcestershire sauce, and hot sauce
lend flavor and spirit to this chunky shrimp dip. To
save preparation time, buy 2¼ pounds of raw peeled,
deveined shrimp instead of peeling and deveining the
3 pounds of shrimp yourself. Or better yet, buy
1½ pounds of cooked, peeled shrimp, and forgo cooking it altogether.*

9 cups water
3 pounds unpeeled medium-size fresh
    shrimp
1 (8-ounce) package cream cheese, softened
3 tablespoons mayonnaise or salad dressing
2 tablespoons fresh lemon juice
1 teaspoon Worcestershire sauce
4 drops of hot sauce
½ teaspoon salt
¼ teaspoon pepper
½ cup minced green onions

Bring water to a boil; add shrimp, and cook
3 to 5 minutes or until shrimp turn pink. Drain
well; rinse with cold water. Cover and chill. Peel
shrimp, and devein, if desired. Chop shrimp; set
aside.
Combine cream cheese and next 6 ingredients; stir well. Stir in shrimp and green onions;
cover and chill 8 hours. Serve with crackers.
Yield: about 4 cups.

Pesto Dip (photo on page 18)

*Prepare a festive array of fresh vegetable crudités to
take a plunge in this intensely flavored dip. Fresh
basil, sharp Parmesan cheese, and mellow pine nuts
flatter the garlicky sour cream base.*

¾ cup lightly packed fresh basil leaves
⅓ cup grated Parmesan cheese
¼ cup pine nuts or chopped walnuts, toasted
3 tablespoons olive oil
1 small clove garlic, minced
¼ teaspoon salt
¼ teaspoon pepper
1 (8-ounce) carton sour cream

Combine all ingredients except sour cream in
container of an electric blender. Process until
smooth, stopping once to scrape down sides. Stir
in sour cream. Serve with fresh vegetables. **Yield:**
1½ cups.

Black Bean Salsa

*So simple, so make-ahead, so scrumptious—this
salsa has it all. Fresh cilantro, lime juice, and cumin
star with black beans against a crisp tortilla chip
backdrop.*

1 (15-ounce) can black beans, rinsed and
    drained
2 tomatoes, chopped
4 green onions, sliced
1 clove garlic, crushed
3 tablespoons chopped fresh cilantro or
    1 tablespoon dried cilantro
2½ tablespoons vegetable oil
2 tablespoons fresh lime juice
½ teaspoon ground cumin
¼ teaspoon salt
¼ teaspoon pepper

Combine all ingredients in a bowl; cover and
chill 8 hours. Drain. Serve with tortilla chips.
Yield: 3 cups.

Festive Cheese
Ball

Festive Cheese Balls

This trio of cheese balls is set to satisfy a hungry party crowd, but if you have a more intimate gathering in mind, store two in the freezer until your next celebration. Better yet, wrap the cheese balls in plastic wrap, and tie with a pretty ribbon for gift giving.

1 (16-ounce) loaf process cheese spread, cubed and softened
4 cups (1 pound) shredded sharp Cheddar cheese, softened
1 (8-ounce) package cream cheese, softened
½ cup chopped pecans or walnuts, toasted
4 cloves garlic, minced
2 tablespoons paprika
½ cup minced fresh parsley

Combine first 3 ingredients, stirring until blended. Stir in pecans and garlic. Divide mixture into 3 equal portions, and shape into balls. Roll each ball in paprika and parsley. Serve with party bread slices or crackers. **Yield:** three 4-inch cheese balls.

NOTE: For a subtly different flavor and appearance, roll the cheese balls in ½ cup toasted chopped pecans or walnuts and ½ cup minced fresh parsley.

Four-Cheese Pâté

Cream cheese, Camembert, blue, and Swiss harmonize in this appetizing cheese pâté. Succulent apple and pear wedges provide sweet accompaniment.

3 (8-ounce) packages cream cheese, softened and divided
2 tablespoons milk
2 tablespoons sour cream
¾ cup chopped pecans, toasted
1 (4½-ounce) package Camembert cheese, softened
1 (4-ounce) package crumbled blue cheese, softened
1 cup (4 ounces) shredded Swiss cheese, softened
Garnish: pecan halves

Line a 9-inch pieplate or cakepan with plastic wrap; set aside. Combine 1 package cream cheese, milk, and sour cream in a mixing bowl; beat at medium speed of an electric mixer until smooth. Spoon mixture into prepared pieplate; spread evenly to edge. Sprinkle with chopped pecans.

Combine remaining 2 packages cream cheese, Camembert cheese (including rind), blue cheese, and Swiss cheese in a mixing bowl; beat at medium speed until smooth. Spoon mixture over chopped pecans in pieplate; spread evenly to edge. Cover and chill at least 2 hours. Invert onto serving plate; carefully remove plastic wrap. Garnish, if desired. Serve with apple wedges and pear slices. **Yield:** 4½ cups.

NOTE: You can make this spread ahead, and store it in the refrigerator up to 1 week.

Red and Blacks

A green onion-studded cream cheese blend encased in brilliant red tomato shells cushions salty beads of black caviar.

24 cherry tomatoes
1 (8-ounce) package cream cheese, softened
¼ cup mayonnaise
⅓ cup finely chopped green onions
1 (3½-ounce) jar black caviar, drained

Cut a thin slice from tops of tomatoes; carefully scoop out pulp, and reserve for another use. Place shells upside down on paper towels.

Combine cream cheese, mayonnaise, and green onions in a small mixing bowl; beat at low speed of an electric mixer until blended. Spoon or pipe mixture into tomato shells. Top each stuffed tomato with a small amount of caviar. Serve with remaining caviar. **Yield:** 2 dozen.

Barbecued Pecans

2 tablespoons butter or margarine, melted
¼ cup Worcestershire sauce
1 tablespoon ketchup
⅛ teaspoon hot sauce
4 cups pecan halves
Salt (optional)

Combine first 4 ingredients in a bowl; stir in pecans. Spread mixture evenly in a 15- x 10- x 1-inch jellyroll pan. Bake at 300° for 30 minutes, stirring often. Drain on paper towels. Sprinkle with salt, if desired. **Yield:** 4 cups.

Antipasto Spread

1 (14-ounce) can artichoke hearts, drained and diced
2 (4-ounce) cans sliced mushrooms, drained and diced
1 (3-ounce) jar pimiento-stuffed olives, drained and diced
½ cup diced ripe olives
½ cup diced celery
¼ cup diced green bell pepper
½ cup white vinegar
½ cup olive oil
¼ cup dried onion flakes
2 tablespoons sugar
2½ teaspoons dry Italian salad dressing mix
½ teaspoon pepper
¼ teaspoon seasoned salt
¼ teaspoon garlic powder
¼ teaspoon onion powder
Leaf lettuce (optional)
1 medium eggplant (optional)

Combine first 6 ingredients in a bowl; set aside.

Combine vinegar and next 8 ingredients in a heavy saucepan; bring to a boil, stirring often. Remove from heat, and immediately pour over reserved vegetables, stirring well. Cover and chill 3 to 4 hours. Spoon spread into a lettuce-lined eggplant bowl, if desired. Serve with bagel chips. **Yield:** 4 cups.

NOTE: To make an eggplant bowl, slice off the top one-third of the eggplant; discard top. Scoop out the pulp, leaving a ½-inch-thick shell.

Red and
Blacks

Party Pastries
(page 32)

Antipasto Spread

Chutney
Spread

Chutney Spread

A supple cream cheese base is ornamented with chutney, green onions, and peanuts, and then showered with a flurry of coconut.

1 (8-ounce) package cream cheese, softened
1 (9-ounce) jar chutney
½ cup sliced green onions
½ cup coarsely chopped dry roasted peanuts
½ cup flaked coconut
Garnish: candied cherry wedges

Spread cream cheese into a 7½-inch circle on a serving plate. Spread chutney over cream cheese; top with green onions and peanuts. Sprinkle coconut in center. Garnish, if desired. Serve immediately or cover and chill up to 1 hour. Serve with crackers or toasted bread cut with Christmas cookie cutters. **Yield:** 3½ cups.

Hot Pepper Jelly Turnovers

1 cup all-purpose flour
1 (5-ounce) jar sharp process cheese spread
½ cup butter or margarine
1 tablespoon cold water
2 tablespoons hot red or green pepper jelly, divided

Place flour in a bowl; cut in cheese spread and butter with pastry blender until mixture is crumbly. Sprinkle cold water evenly over surface; stir with a fork until dry ingredients are moistened. Shape into a ball; cover and chill at least 4 hours.

Divide dough in half; keep 1 portion chilled. Roll remaining portion to ¼-inch thickness on a heavily floured surface. Cut into rounds with a 3-inch biscuit cutter; place ¼ teaspoon jelly in center of each round. Moisten edges with water. Fold each round in half, and press edges with a fork to seal (edges must be well sealed). Place on lightly greased baking sheets. Repeat procedure with remaining portion of dough. Bake at 375° for 10 to 12 minutes or until lightly browned. Transfer to wire racks to cool. **Yield:** about 2 dozen.

Hot Pepper
Jelly Turnovers

Curried Party Mix

3 cups bite-size crispy corn cereal squares*
3 cups bite-size crispy wheat cereal squares*
1½ cups cashews
1 cup flaked coconut
½ cup butter or margarine, melted
1 to 1½ teaspoons curry powder
Dash of ground red pepper
1 cup dried banana chips
1 cup raisins

Combine first 4 ingredients in a large bowl; set aside. Combine butter, curry powder, and ground red pepper; pour over cereal mixture. Toss to coat evenly.

Spread mixture in an ungreased 15- x 10- x 1-inch jellyroll pan. Bake at 250° for 45 minutes, stirring every 15 minutes; stir in banana chips and raisins during last 15 minutes of baking. Cool completely; store in an airtight container. Yield: 10 cups.

* For cereal squares, we used Corn Chex and Wheat Chex brands.

Cheese Christmas Trees (photo on page 35)

2 cups (8 ounces) shredded Cheddar cheese
1 cup butter or margarine, softened
½ teaspoon salt
⅛ teaspoon ground red pepper
2 cups all-purpose flour
½ teaspoon lemon juice
Paprika

Beat first 4 ingredients in a large mixing bowl at medium speed of an electric mixer; stir in flour and lemon juice.

Fill a cookie gun or press fitted with a tree-shaped disc; follow manufacturer's directions, pressing onto ungreased baking sheets.

Bake at 325° for 15 minutes. Sprinkle with paprika. Store in an airtight container or, if desired, freeze up to 3 months. Yield: 5½ dozen.

Mushroom Tarts

2 tablespoons butter or margarine
¾ cup chopped onion
1 pound fresh mushrooms, chopped
1 tablespoon lemon juice
½ teaspoon salt
Pinch of pepper
1 tablespoon cornstarch
1 tablespoon water
1 cup whipping cream
Tart Shells
¼ cup (1 ounce) shredded Gruyère
    cheese

Melt butter in a skillet over medium heat; add onion, and cook, stirring constantly, until tender. Stir in mushrooms; cook, stirring constantly, 8 to 10 minutes or until liquid evaporates. Stir in lemon juice, salt, and pepper; set aside.

Combine cornstarch and water in a saucepan; stir in whipping cream. Cook over low heat, stirring constantly, until thickened and bubbly. Stir sauce into mushroom mixture.

Fill shells evenly with filling; sprinkle with cheese. Place on ungreased baking sheets. Bake at 400° for 10 minutes or until cheese melts. Yield: 3 dozen.

Tart Shells

2 cups all-purpose flour
1 teaspoon salt
¾ cup butter or margarine
¼ cup cold water

Combine flour and salt; cut in butter with pastry blender until mixture is crumbly. Sprinkle cold water, 1 tablespoon at a time, evenly over surface; stir with a fork until dry ingredients are moistened. Shape into a ball; cover and chill.

Divide dough into 36 balls. Place balls in ungreased miniature (1¾-inch) muffin pans, pressing dough on bottom and up sides to form shells. Bake at 425° for 10 minutes or until lightly browned. Remove from pans, and cool 5 minutes on wire racks. Yield: 3 dozen.

Vegetable Stuffed Mushrooms

Vegetable Stuffed Mushrooms

Cream cheese with merry morsels of celery, radishes, and onion fills fresh mushroom caps to the brim with sprightly appeal.

36 medium-size fresh mushrooms
2 (3-ounce) packages cream cheese,
     softened
⅓ cup sour cream
¼ cup minced celery
¼ cup minced radishes
¼ cup minced fresh parsley
2 tablespoons minced onion
1 teaspoon lemon juice
¼ teaspoon salt
¼ teaspoon ground white pepper
Garnishes: sliced radishes, fresh parsley
     sprigs

Clean mushrooms with damp paper towels. Remove mushroom stems, and reserve stems for another use.

Combine softened cream cheese and sour cream in a small mixing bowl; beat at medium speed of an electric mixer until mixture is smooth. Add celery and next 6 ingredients, stirring gently to combine.

Spoon cream cheese mixture evenly into mushroom caps. Cover and chill. Garnish, if desired. **Yield:** 3 dozen.

Cherry-Sauced Meatballs

2 cups loosely packed torn white bread
½ cup milk
1 tablespoon soy sauce
1 teaspoon garlic salt
¼ teaspoon onion powder
½ pound lean ground beef
½ pound hot ground pork sausage
1 (8-ounce) can sliced water chestnuts,
    drained and chopped
Cherry Sauce

Combine first 5 ingredients, stirring well. Combine ground beef and sausage; add to bread mixture, stirring well. Stir in water chestnuts.

Shape mixture into ¾-inch balls. Place on a lightly greased rack in broiler pan; bake at 350° for 20 minutes.

Place meatballs in chafing dish; add Cherry Sauce, stirring gently to coat. Serve with wooden picks. **Yield:** 4 dozen.

Cherry Sauce
1 (21-ounce) can cherry pie filling
⅓ cup dry sherry
¼ cup white vinegar
¼ cup steak sauce
2 tablespoons brown sugar
2 tablespoons soy sauce

Combine all ingredients in a medium saucepan. Cook over medium heat, stirring constantly, until thoroughly heated. **Yield:** about 2½ cups.

Flank Steak Rolls with Horseradish Sauce

1 (1-ounce) envelope onion soup mix
½ cup vegetable oil
¼ cup white vinegar
1 tablespoon Worcestershire sauce
½ teaspoon sugar
3 pounds flank steak
Horseradish Sauce
Party rolls

Combine first 5 ingredients in a shallow dish; stir well. Add steak, turning to coat. Cover and marinate in refrigerator 8 hours, turning once.

Remove steak from marinade, reserving marinade. Bring marinade to a boil; remove from heat. Grill steak over hot coals about 10 minutes on each side or to desired degree of doneness, basting often with marinade.

Slice steak across grain into thin slices. Serve with Horseradish Sauce on party rolls. **Yield:** 30 appetizer servings.

Horseradish Sauce
2 teaspoons prepared horseradish
½ teaspoon minced fresh dill
¼ teaspoon garlic salt
¾ cup whipping cream, whipped
Garnish: fresh dill sprig

Fold first 3 ingredients into whipped cream. Spoon into a serving dish. Garnish, if desired. **Yield:** about 1½ cups.

Pork Tenderloin Appetizer Sandwiches

(photo on page 18)

Tender pork is steeped in a spiced red wine mixture, roasted to perfection, and then sliced and swathed in a blanket of spicy mayonnaise on party rolls.

½ cup dry red wine
2 tablespoons olive oil
1½ tablespoons Worcestershire sauce
1 teaspoon dried thyme
¾ teaspoon onion powder
½ teaspoon cumin seeds
¼ teaspoon pepper
⅛ teaspoon garlic powder
⅛ teaspoon ground cloves
1 (¾-pound) pork tenderloin
¼ cup mayonnaise
¼ cup spicy brown mustard
Party rolls

Combine first 9 ingredients in a shallow dish; add tenderloin. Cover and marinate in refrigerator 8 hours, turning occasionally.

Remove tenderloin from marinade, reserving marinade. Bring marinade to a boil; set aside. Place meat on a rack in a shallow roasting pan.

Bake, uncovered, at 425° for 30 to 35 minutes or until a meat thermometer inserted in thickest portion registers 160°, basting occasionally with marinade. Let stand 10 minutes.

Combine mayonnaise and mustard, stirring well. Cut tenderloin into ¼-inch slices. Serve with mayonnaise mixture on party rolls. **Yield:** 8 appetizer servings.

Ham Rolls

1 (3-ounce) package cream cheese, softened
2 tablespoons finely chopped green bell pepper
2 tablespoons chopped pimiento
1 tablespoon mayonnaise
1½ teaspoons Creole mustard
6 (6- x 4- x ⅛-inch) slices boiled ham

Combine all ingredients except ham. Spread cream cheese mixture evenly on 1 side of each ham slice; roll up, starting with short end, and secure with a wooden pick. Cover and chill.

Slice each roll into ½-inch pieces; serve with wooden picks. **Yield:** 4 dozen.

Miniature Sausage Quiches

½ pound mild ground pork sausage, cooked and drained
2 large eggs, beaten
½ cup milk
1½ tablespoons butter or margarine, melted
1 cup (4 ounces) shredded Cheddar cheese
Pastry Shells
Paprika
Garnish: fresh parsley sprigs

Combine first 5 ingredients; stir well, and pour into prepared pastry shells. Sprinkle with paprika. Bake at 350° for 20 to 25 minutes or until set. Garnish, if desired. **Yield:** 3 dozen.

Pastry Shells
2 cups all-purpose flour
1 teaspoon salt
⅓ cup butter or margarine, melted
1 egg yolk
5 to 6 tablespoons cold water

Combine flour and salt; add butter and egg yolk, stirring well. Sprinkle cold water (1 tablespoon at a time) evenly over surface; stir with a fork until dry ingredients are moistened. Shape dough into a ball; cover and chill.

Divide dough into 36 balls. Place balls in lightly greased miniature (1¾-inch) muffin pans or assorted canapé tins, pressing dough on bottom and up sides to form shells. Prick bottom and sides of shells with a fork. Bake at 400° for 5 minutes. Remove from pans, and cool on wire racks. **Yield:** 3 dozen.

Miniature Sausage Quiches
Ham Rolls

Party Pastries

½ cup butter or margarine, softened
1 (3-ounce) package cream cheese, softened
1 cup all-purpose flour
Dash of salt
Leaf lettuce
Chicken Salad Filling

Party Pastries

Combine butter and cream cheese in a mixing bowl; beat at medium speed of an electric mixer until smooth. Add flour and salt; mix well.

Divide dough into 30 balls. Place in ungreased miniature (1¾-inch) muffin pans, pressing dough on bottom and up sides to form shells. Prick bottom and sides of shells with a fork. Bake at 400° for 10 minutes or until lightly browned. Remove from pans, and cool on wire racks.

Line shells with lettuce. Spoon Chicken Salad Filling evenly into shells. Cover and chill. **Yield:** 2½ dozen.

Chicken Salad Filling

¾ cup finely chopped cooked chicken
⅓ cup mayonnaise
¼ cup finely chopped celery
2 tablespoons finely chopped green bell pepper
2 tablespoons finely chopped dill pickle
⅛ teaspoon ground white pepper

Combine all ingredients; stir well. Cover and chill. **Yield:** 1½ cups.

NOTE: For a change of pace, make a pizza filling for these pastries instead of chicken salad. You'll need ⅓ cup pizza sauce and ½ cup (2 ounces) shredded mozzarella cheese (omit the lettuce). Simply spoon the pizza sauce evenly into the shells, and top with cheese. Bake at 350° for 5 minutes or until cheese melts. Serve warm.

Party Pizzas

These spicy little bites are perfect for a crowd or, when stored in the freezer, a hungry family who wants a quick snack.

1 pound hot ground pork sausage
1 (16-ounce) loaf process cheese spread, diced
¼ cup ketchup
2 tablespoons Worcestershire sauce
1 teaspoon dried oregano
1 teaspoon fennel seeds
1 (16-ounce) loaf cocktail rye bread

Brown sausage in a large skillet, stirring until it crumbles; drain well. Add cheese spread and next 4 ingredients; cook over medium heat, stirring constantly, until cheese spread melts. Spread mixture evenly on bread slices; place on ungreased baking sheets. Bake at 350° for 10 minutes or until bubbly. **Yield:** about 6 dozen.

NOTE: To make Party Pizzas ahead, place the unbaked pizzas in a single layer on large baking sheets, and freeze until firm. Place the pizzas in plastic freezer bags. To serve, thaw and bake as directed.

Spicy Chicken Bites

Chunks of tender chicken wrapped in a crispy cracker coating take a dunk in a pool of buttery brown mustard, dry sherry, and soy sauce.

¾ cup butter or margarine, melted and
    divided
½ cup spicy brown mustard, divided
4 skinned and boned chicken breast halves,
    cut into bite-size pieces
1 cup saltine cracker crumbs
2 tablespoons dry sherry
1 tablespoon soy sauce
⅛ teaspoon garlic powder

Combine ¼ cup melted butter and ¼ cup mustard; stir well. Dip chicken pieces in mustard mixture, and dredge in cracker crumbs. Place chicken in an ungreased 13- x 9- x 2 inch pan; drizzle with ¼ cup melted butter. Bake, uncovered, at 375° for 20 to 25 minutes or until lightly browned. Drain on paper towels.

Combine remaining ¼ cup melted butter, remaining ¼ cup mustard, sherry, soy sauce, and garlic powder; stir well. Serve chicken with sauce. **Yield:** about 30 appetizers.

Taco Chicken Drummettes

1½ pounds chicken drummettes
1 (8-ounce) jar hot taco sauce
1 cup dry breadcrumbs
3 tablespoons taco seasoning mix

Combine drummettes and taco sauce in a shallow dish; cover and chill 2 hours.

Combine breadcrumbs and seasoning mix in a shallow bowl. Dredge drummettes in breadcrumb mixture, and place on a lightly greased baking sheet. Bake at 375° for 35 to 40 minutes. **Yield:** 16 drummettes.

Little Crab Cream Puffs

1 cup water
½ cup butter or margarine
1 cup all-purpose flour
¼ teaspoon salt
4 large eggs
3 (6-ounce) cans crabmeat, drained and
    flaked
1 cup (4 ounces) shredded Cheddar cheese
½ cup finely chopped celery
½ cup chopped ripe olives
½ cup mayonnaise
2 tablespoons finely chopped green onions
1 teaspoon grated lemon rind
Dash of garlic powder

Bring water and butter to a boil over medium heat; reduce heat to low. Add flour and salt, and beat with a wooden spoon until mixture leaves sides of pan. Remove from heat, and cool slightly. Add eggs, one at a time, beating until mixture is smooth.

Drop batter by teaspoonfuls onto lightly greased baking sheets. Bake at 425° for 10 minutes; reduce heat to 325°, and bake 8 to 10 additional minutes or until puffed and golden. Turn oven off. Pierce warm puffs on 1 side with a small sharp knife to let steam escape, and leave in oven 10 minutes to dry out. Remove cream puffs from oven, and transfer to wire racks to cool completely. Slice top one-third from each cream puff, and reserve.

Combine crabmeat and remaining 7 ingredients; stir well. Spoon 1 tablespoon crabmeat mixture into each cream puff; replace tops. Place puffs on ungreased baking sheets. Bake at 250° for 15 minutes or until thoroughly heated. Serve immediately. **Yield:** 4 dozen.

NOTE: If you prefer fresh crabmeat, substitute 1 pound of fresh crabmeat that has been drained and flaked for the canned variety.

Sparkling Raspberry
Punch (page 38)

Cheese Christmas
Trees (page 27)

Holiday Spirits

Beverages

*W*hether you're coming in
from the cold for a warming mugful of
hot chocolate, welcoming holiday
guests with a cup of velvety eggnog, or
toasting the New Year with a flute of
bubbly punch, we have the season's best
beverage recipes to share with you.

Spiced Apple Cider

A spicy bundle brimming with cloves, allspice, and orange rind simmers in this apple cider and fruit juice mixture. This seasonal pleasure is at home served warm or chilled at holiday gatherings.

1 teaspoon whole cloves
½ teaspoon whole allspice
Rind of 1 orange, cut into strips
2 quarts apple cider
3 cups pineapple juice
¾ cup orange juice
2 tablespoons lemon juice

Place first 3 ingredients in a cheesecloth bag; combine spice bag, cider, and remaining ingredients in a Dutch oven. Cook, uncovered, over medium heat until thoroughly heated. Remove and discard spice bag. Serve warm or chilled. **Yield:** about 3 quarts.

Hot Cranberry Tea

This sweetly spiced brew of cranberry, orange, and lemon juice is guaranteed to warm your spirits.

3½ quarts water
4 cups fresh cranberries
12 whole cloves
4 (3-inch) sticks cinnamon
2 cups sugar
Juice of 2 oranges (⅔ cup)
Juice of 2 lemons (¼ cup)

Combine first 4 ingredients in a Dutch oven. Bring to a boil; cover, reduce heat, and simmer 12 minutes. Pour mixture through several layers of cheesecloth in a wire-mesh strainer into a large container, discarding cheesecloth, cranberries, and spices. Return mixture to pan. Add sugar and remaining ingredients, stirring until sugar dissolves. Serve warm. **Yield:** 3½ quarts.

Holiday Cheer

2 (750-milliliter) bottles rosé wine, chilled
2 cups port
1 cup cherry brandy
Juice of 2 oranges (⅔ cup)
Juice of 2 lemons (¼ cup)
½ cup superfine sugar
1 (1-liter) bottle club soda, chilled

Combine first 5 ingredients; add sugar, stirring until sugar dissolves. Stir in club soda just before serving. Serve over crushed ice. **Yield:** 3 quarts.

Holiday Cheer

Orange Wassail

Wassail is Scandinavian for "be in good health." Make two batches of this traditional drink, one with bourbon and one without, so that merrymakers, young and young-at-heart, can benefit from a toast to good health.

1 (64-ounce) carton orange juice
1 (64-ounce) bottle apple juice
1 (32-ounce) bottle cranberry juice cocktail
1 (12-ounce) can frozen lemonade
     concentrate, thawed and undiluted
1 (2-inch) stick cinnamon
3 cups bourbon (optional)
1 tablespoon whole cloves
2 oranges, sliced

Combine first 5 ingredients in a large Dutch oven. Stir in bourbon, if desired. Insert cloves into orange slices; add to juice mixture. Cook, uncovered, over medium heat until thoroughly heated. Serve warm. **Yield:** 6 quarts.

Spicy Bloody Mary

1 (46-ounce) can tomato juice
1 (10½-ounce) can condensed beef broth,
    undiluted
¼ cup Worcestershire sauce
2 tablespoons lime juice
1½ teaspoons seasoned salt
1½ teaspoons celery salt
1 teaspoon instant minced onion
1 teaspoon celery seeds
½ teaspoon freshly ground pepper
3 or 4 dashes of hot sauce
1 to 2 cups vodka
Garnish: celery stalks

Combine all ingredients except vodka and celery stalks; chill. Stir in vodka just before serving. Garnish, if desired. **Yield:** 2 quarts.

Citrus Punch

1 (46-ounce) can pineapple juice
1 (46-ounce) can apple juice
1 (12-ounce) can frozen lemonade
    concentrate, thawed and undiluted
½ cup sugar
4 (1-liter) bottles ginger ale, chilled
Citrus Ice Ring (optional)

Combine first 4 ingredients, stirring until sugar dissolves. Pour juice mixture evenly into four heavy-duty, zip-top plastic bags; seal securely. Freeze until firm.

Thaw juice mixture in a punch bowl until slushy as needed, adding 1 bottle ginger ale to each bag of fruit juice mixture; stir gently. Add Citrus Ice Ring, if desired. **Yield:** 7½ quarts.

Citrus Ice Ring
6 cups bottled or boiled, cooled water
Oranges, limes, lemons

Pour 3 cups water into a 6-cup ring mold; freeze. Set remaining water aside.

For each citrus rose, cut a thin slice from bottom of fruit, using a sharp paring knife; discard slice. Beginning at top of fruit, peel a continuous ½- to ¾-inch-wide strip. Starting with first portion cut, coil strip to look like a rose, coiling tightly at first to form center, and gradually coiling more loosely to form outer petals. Secure with wooden picks.

Arrange citrus roses on top of ice ring. Slowly fill mold with reserved water (citrus roses will float). Partially freeze ice ring; remove wooden picks from citrus roses, and return ice ring to freezer until firm. Let stand at room temperature 5 minutes. Carefully remove ice ring from mold. **Yield:** 1 ice ring.

Champagne Punch
with Ice Ring

Champagne Punch with Ice Ring

In a hurry? Use one 20-ounce can unsweetened pineapple chunks, drained, instead of fresh pineapple.

6   cups bottled or boiled, cooled water
Fresh strawberries, kiwifruit slices, kumquat
        halves
1   fresh pineapple, cut into bite-size pieces
2½ cups sugar, divided
1¾ cups lemon juice
1   (750-milliliter) bottle champagne, chilled
1   (750-milliliter) bottle dry white wine,
        chilled
2   quarts cold water

Pour 4½ cups water into a 6-cup ring mold; freeze. Arrange strawberries, kiwifruit, and kumquats on top of ice, letting fruit extend above top of mold. Pour remaining 1½ cups water over fruit, filling mold to within ½ inch of top; freeze.

Combine pineapple and 1 cup sugar; let stand at room temperature 30 minutes.

Combine lemon juice and remaining 1½ cups sugar, stirring until sugar dissolves.

To serve, combine pineapple mixture, lemon juice mixture, champagne, wine, and cold water in a punch bowl. Let ice ring stand at room temperature 5 minutes. Carefully remove ice ring from mold, and place in punch bowl, fruit side up. **Yield:** 4½ quarts.

Party Punch

½ cup water
3   tablespoons sugar
3   tablespoons red cinnamon candies
1   (46-ounce) can pineapple juice
1   (2-liter) bottle raspberry-flavored ginger
        ale, chilled

Combine first 3 ingredients in a saucepan; cook over medium heat 5 minutes, stirring constantly, until sugar and candy dissolve. Let cool.

Combine sugar mixture and pineapple juice; chill at least 2 hours. Stir in ginger ale just before serving. Serve over ice. **Yield:** 3½ quarts.

Sparkling Raspberry Punch (photo on page 34)

2   (10-ounce) packages frozen raspberries
        without syrup, thawed
1   (6-ounce) can frozen pink lemonade
        concentrate, thawed and undiluted
¼ cup sugar
1   (1-liter) bottle white Zinfandel wine
1   (2-liter) bottle raspberry-flavored ginger ale
        or ginger ale, chilled

Combine first 3 ingredients in container of an electric blender; process until smooth. Pour mixture through a large wire-mesh strainer into a large container, discarding seeds. Combine raspberry mixture and wine; chill 2 hours. Stir in ginger ale just before serving. **Yield:** 6 quarts.

Coffee Punch

Coffee Punch

*A triple jolt of java ignites this thick, frothy punch.
Brewed coffee, coffee ice cream, and coffee-flavored
liqueur comprise the delightful blend.*

¾ cup freshly ground coffee
2 quarts water
2 cups coffee ice cream, softened
1 cup vanilla ice cream, softened
½ cup Kahlúa or other coffee-flavored
        liqueur
½ cup brandy
⅓ cup sugar (optional)
2 cups coffee ice cream
1 cup vanilla ice cream
1 cup whipping cream
2 tablespoons powdered sugar
Ground cinnamon

Prepare coffee according to manufacturer's
directions, using ¾ cup freshly ground coffee and
2 quarts water. Cool.

Combine coffee, 2 cups softened coffee ice
cream, and next 3 ingredients in a large mixing
bowl. Add ⅓ cup sugar, if desired, and beat at
medium speed of an electric mixer until smooth.
Pour coffee mixture into a punch bowl.

Scoop 2 cups coffee ice cream and 1 cup
vanilla ice cream into coffee mixture.

Combine whipping cream and powdered
sugar; beat at medium speed until soft peaks
form. Dollop over coffee mixture, and sprinkle
with cinnamon. **Yield:** about 3½ quarts.

Mocha Eggnog

Mocha Eggnog

Eggnog gets a holiday makeover with instant coffee granules, chocolate syrup, and brandy.

1½ tablespoons instant coffee granules
½ cup hot water
1 (32-ounce) carton refrigerated eggnog
¼ to ½ cup brandy (optional)
½ cup chocolate syrup
½ cup whipping cream, whipped
Garnish: grated semisweet chocolate

Dissolve instant coffee granules in hot water; let cool. Combine coffee, eggnog, brandy, if desired, and chocolate syrup; cover and chill thoroughly.

Fold in whipped cream just before serving. Garnish, if desired. **Yield:** about 1½ quarts.

Fireside Chocolate

4 cups milk
5 (1-ounce) squares semisweet chocolate, chopped
2 (3-inch) sticks cinnamon
1 teaspoon vanilla extract
Whipped cream (optional)
Ground cinnamon (optional)

Combine first 4 ingredients in a large saucepan; cook over medium heat, stirring constantly, until chocolate melts and mixture is thoroughly heated. Remove and discard cinnamon sticks.

Beat at high speed of an electric mixer 1 to 2 minutes. Pour into mugs. If desired, top each serving with whipped cream, and sprinkle with cinnamon. **Yield:** 4½ cups.

Holiday Hot Chocolate

1½ cups sugar
½ cup cocoa
⅛ teaspoon salt
5 cups water
1 (12-ounce) can evaporated milk
2 cups milk
Sweetened whipped cream
Crushed peppermint candy

Combine first 3 ingredients in a large Dutch oven; stir well. Gradually stir in water; bring to a boil. Add evaporated milk and milk; cook until thoroughly heated, stirring occasionally. Pour into mugs. Top each serving with whipped cream, and sprinkle with crushed candy. **Yield:** 7 cups.

NOTE: For a spiked version, add ¾ cup peppermint schnapps to this hot chocolate mixture just before serving.

Cappuccino

3 cups strongly brewed coffee
3 cups half-and-half
½ cup crème de cacao
¼ cup rum
¼ cup brandy
Sugar (optional)

Combine all ingredients in a saucepan; cook over medium heat until hot, stirring occasionally. Serve immediately. **Yield:** 1¾ quarts.

Kahlúa Coffee

6 cups strongly brewed coffee
¾ cup chocolate syrup
¼ cup Kahlúa or other coffee-flavored liqueur
¼ teaspoon almond extract
½ cup whipping cream, whipped

Combine coffee, chocolate syrup, Kahlúa, and almond extract in a large saucepan; cook over medium heat until hot, stirring occasionally. Serve immediately. Top each serving with a dollop of whipped cream. **Yield:** 7 cups.

Spiced Coffee

6 cups cold water
4 (3-inch) sticks cinnamon
¾ cup freshly ground coffee
8 whole allspice
8 whole cloves
Honey (optional)

Place cold water and cinnamon sticks in bottom of an electric percolator. Place coffee, allspice, and cloves in percolator basket. Perk through complete cycle of percolator. Serve warm with honey, if desired. **Yield:** 6 cups.

Fresh Lemon
Muffins (page 48)

Gumdrop Wreath Bread
(page 52)

Panettone
(page 53)

Santa's Bakeshop

Breads

Fill your kitchen with holiday warmth by baking bread—the enticing aroma will waft through your home, kindling spirits and creating special memories. Our choices take you from breakfast breads brimming with fruit and nuts, to dinner rolls ornamented with herbs and cheese, to delightful desserts dripping with icicles of sweet glaze.

Jelly-Filled
Doughnuts
(page 55)

Bran Muffins with
Honey-Nut Butter

Almond Twists
(page 55)

Bran Muffins with Honey-Nut Butter

If you need a jump on breakfast during the hectic holiday season, try this recipe. You can bake a batch of muffins whenever you like, because the batter can be stored in the refrigerator up to five days.

1¼ cups bran cereal with raisins, peaches, and almonds*
1 cup buttermilk
¼ cup vegetable oil
1 large egg, lightly beaten
1¼ cups all-purpose flour
1 teaspoon baking soda
¼ teaspoon salt
½ cup sugar
Honey-Nut Butter

Combine cereal and buttermilk in a bowl; let stand 5 minutes. Add oil and egg; stir well.

Combine flour and next 3 ingredients in a large bowl; make a well in center of mixture. Add cereal mixture to dry ingredients, stirring just until moistened.

Spoon batter into a greased muffin pan, filling three-fourths full. Bake at 400° for 18 minutes. Remove from pan immediately. Serve with Honey-Nut Butter. **Yield:** 1 dozen.

Honey-Nut Butter
½ cup butter or margarine, softened
¼ cup honey
3 tablespoons chopped almonds or pecans, toasted

Beat butter at medium speed of an electric mixer until creamy; gradually add honey, beating until blended. Stir in almonds. Store in refrigerator. **Yield:** about 1 cup.

* For bran cereal with raisins, peaches, and almonds, we used Fruit and Fiber brand.

NOTE: Make 3 dozen mini-muffins by spooning the batter evenly into greased miniature (1¾-inch) muffin pans. Bake at 400° for 15 minutes.

Pumpkin Muffins

These versatile spiced muffins take you from fall to winter with finesse. Make them as a Halloween treat, and pop the remaining muffins in the freezer. You can freeze them up to three months.

4 cups all-purpose flour
1¾ teaspoons baking soda
½ teaspoon baking powder
1 teaspoon salt
2¾ cups sugar
1¼ cups raisins
¾ cup chopped walnuts
1 tablespoon ground cinnamon
1 tablespoon ground nutmeg
1 tablespoon ground cloves
4 large eggs, lightly beaten
2½ cups canned pumpkin
1 cup vegetable oil
1 cup water

Combine first 10 ingredients in a large bowl; make a well in center of mixture. Combine eggs and remaining 3 ingredients; add to dry ingredients, stirring just until moistened.

Spoon batter into paper-lined muffin pans, filling two-thirds full. Bake at 375° for 20 minutes. Remove from pans immediately. **Yield:** 3½ dozen.

Fresh Lemon Muffins (photo on page 42)

½ cup butter or margarine, softened
½ cup sugar
2 large eggs
1 tablespoon grated lemon rind
3 tablespoons fresh lemon juice
1 cup all-purpose flour
1 teaspoon baking powder
⅛ teaspoon salt
2 tablespoons sugar
¼ teaspoon ground cinnamon

Beat butter at medium speed of an electric mixer until creamy; gradually add ½ cup sugar, beating well. Add eggs, one at a time, beating after each addition. Stir in lemon rind and juice.

Combine flour, baking powder, and salt; add to butter mixture, beating well.

Spoon batter into greased miniature (1¾-inch) muffin pans, filling two-thirds full. Combine 2 tablespoons sugar and cinnamon; sprinkle evenly over batter. Bake at 375° for 15 minutes. Remove from pans immediately. **Yield:** 2½ dozen.

Eggnog Pancakes

Start a new tradition by serving these eggnog-laced pancakes Christmas morning. A hint of nutmeg and cloves permeates each tender bite.

1⅓ cups all-purpose flour
¼ cup sugar
1 teaspoon baking soda
½ teaspoon salt
¼ teaspoon ground nutmeg
⅛ teaspoon ground cloves
1½ cups refrigerated eggnog
1 large egg, lightly beaten
1 tablespoon vegetable oil

Combine first 6 ingredients in a large bowl. Combine eggnog, egg, and oil; add to flour mixture, stirring just until dry ingredients are moistened.

Pour about ¼ cup batter for each pancake onto a hot, lightly greased griddle or skillet. Cook pancakes until tops are covered with bubbles and edges look cooked; turn and cook other side. **Yield:** 12 (4-inch) pancakes.

NOTE: These pancakes freeze and reheat with great results. Simply stack the cooked pancakes between sheets of wax paper, place in an airtight container, and freeze up to a month. To reheat, place the frozen pancakes in a single layer on a baking sheet. Bake at 325° for 10 minutes.

Granola Pancakes

This hearty interpretation of buttermilk pancakes calls on whole wheat flour, granola, and cinnamon for its homespun goodness.

½ cup all-purpose flour
½ cup whole wheat flour
1½ teaspoons baking powder
½ teaspoon baking soda
⅓ cup oats and honey granola cereal with almonds*
1 tablespoon flaked coconut
½ teaspoon ground cinnamon
1 large egg, beaten
1 cup plus 2 tablespoons buttermilk
1 tablespoon vegetable oil

Combine first 7 ingredients in a large bowl. Combine egg, buttermilk, and oil; add to flour mixture, stirring just until dry ingredients are moistened.

Pour about ¼ cup batter for each pancake onto a hot, lightly greased griddle or skillet. Cook pancakes until tops are covered with bubbles and edges look cooked; turn and cook other side. **Yield:** 8 (4-inch) pancakes.

* For oats and honey granola cereal with almonds, we used Quaker 100% Natural Oats & Honey Cereal.

Buttermilk
Waffles

Buttermilk Waffles

Whipped egg whites folded in these buttermilk waffles keep them extra light and crisp. Every pocket of these golden waffles is ready and waiting to soak in melting Orange Butter.

5¼ cups all-purpose flour
1 tablespoon plus 2 teaspoons baking
      powder
1¼ teaspoons baking soda
½ teaspoon salt
5 large eggs, separated
3½ cups buttermilk
1 cup vegetable oil
Orange Butter
Honey
Garnishes: chopped pecans, orange slices,
      fresh strawberries

Combine first 4 ingredients in a large bowl, stirring well. Beat egg yolks; add beaten egg yolks, buttermilk, and oil to flour mixture, stirring until blended.

Beat egg whites at high speed of an electric mixer until soft peaks form; fold into batter.

Pour about 1¼ cups batter for each waffle into a hot, lightly oiled waffle iron, spreading batter almost to edges. Cook 5 minutes or until done. Serve with Orange Butter and honey. Garnish, if desired. **Yield:** 20 (4-inch) waffles.

Orange Butter
1 cup butter or margarine, softened
¼ cup sifted powdered sugar
2 tablespoons grated orange rind
¼ cup orange juice

Beat first 3 ingredients at medium speed of an electric mixer until fluffy; gradually add orange juice, beating until blended. Serve at room temperature. Store in refrigerator. **Yield:** 1¼ cups.

Chocolate-Filled Coffee Ring

You can make this chocolaty coffee ring ahead and freeze it up to three months. On Christmas morning, warm up the bread, and drizzle on the glaze.

1 package active dry yeast
¼ cup warm water (105° to 115°)
¾ cup milk
⅓ cup butter or margarine
¼ cup sugar
1 teaspoon salt
2 large eggs, beaten
1 teaspoon vanilla extract
3½ to 4 cups all-purpose flour
1 cup (6 ounces) semisweet chocolate
    morsels
½ cup chopped pecans
1 large egg, beaten
2 cups sifted powdered sugar
3 tablespoons milk

Combine yeast and warm water in a 1-cup liquid measuring cup; let stand 5 minutes.

Combine ¾ cup milk and next 3 ingredients in a saucepan; heat until butter melts, stirring occasionally. Cool to 105° to 115°.

Combine yeast mixture, milk mixture, 2 eggs, and vanilla in a large bowl. Gradually stir in enough flour to make a soft dough.

Turn out onto a heavily floured surface, and knead until smooth and elastic (about 8 minutes). Place in a well-greased bowl, turning to grease top. Cover and let rise in a warm place (85°), free from drafts, 1½ hours or until doubled in bulk.

Punch dough down; turn out onto a floured surface, and knead 4 or 5 times. Roll into a 22- x 14-inch rectangle; sprinkle with chocolate morsels and pecans, leaving a 1-inch border.

Roll up, jellyroll fashion, starting at long side; pinch seam to seal. Place roll, seam side down, on a large greased baking sheet; shape into a ring, and pinch ends together to seal.

Cut dough at 1-inch intervals around ring, using a sharp knife or kitchen shears, cutting two-thirds of the way through. Gently turn each piece of dough on its side, slightly overlapping slices. Cover and let rise in a warm place, free from drafts, 1 hour or until doubled in bulk. Gently brush with beaten egg.

Bake at 350° for 25 to 30 minutes or until browned. Remove to a wire rack; cool 15 minutes.

Combine powdered sugar and 3 tablespoons milk; drizzle over warm coffee cake. **Yield:** 1 coffee cake.

NOTE: You can streamline preparation on the front end by using one 16-ounce package of hot roll mix in place of the yeast dough (first 9 ingredients). Prepare the roll mix according to package directions, adding 2 tablespoons sugar. Roll out, and proceed as directed.

YEAST BREAD TIPS

• For traditional yeast breads, dissolve active dry yeast in warm water (105° to 115°). Water that's too hot will kill the yeast, while water that's too cool will make the bread slow to rise. (We recommend dissolving the yeast in a liquid measuring cup instead of a large bowl because the smaller container will retain the heat of the water longer.)
• Some breads follow the rapid-mix method in which the yeast is mixed with dry ingredients before adding the liquid. When using this method, the liquid should be 120° to 130°.
• The ideal rising conditions for yeast bread are an 85° temperature and a draft-free environment. Place the dough in a greased bowl, turning it to coat the surface to prevent a dry skin from forming. Cover the bowl with plastic wrap, then place in a gas oven with a pilot light or an electric oven containing a large pan of hot water.
• To test the dough for doubled bulk, lightly press a finger ½ inch into the dough. If the indention remains, the dough is ready to shape.
• Test for doneness by tapping the loaf with your knuckles and listening for a hollow sound. Aluminum foil may be used to cover the bread if it starts to get too brown before it sounds hollow.

Cranberry Coffee Cake

2 packages active dry yeast
½ cup warm water (105° to 115°)
1 cup milk
½ cup sugar
½ cup sour cream
½ cup butter or margarine
2 large eggs, beaten
2 teaspoons salt
2 teaspoons grated orange rind
5½ to 6 cups all-purpose flour
1 (12-ounce) jar cranberry-orange relish
2 tablespoons chopped pecans
1 cup sifted powdered sugar
1 tablespoon orange juice

Combine yeast in warm water in a 1-cup liquid measuring cup; let stand 5 minutes.

Combine milk and next 3 ingredients in a saucepan; heat until butter melts, stirring occasionally. Cool to 105° to 115°.

Combine yeast mixture, milk mixture, eggs, salt, rind, and 2 cups flour; beat at medium speed of an electric mixer 2 minutes. Gradually stir in enough remaining flour to make a stiff dough. Place in a well-greased bowl, turning to grease top; cover and chill at least 8 hours.

Turn dough out onto a floured surface, and knead until smooth and elastic (about 1 minute). Roll into a 15- x 10-inch rectangle on a floured surface. Spread relish over dough, leaving a 1-inch border; sprinkle with pecans.

Roll up, jellyroll fashion, starting at long side; pinch seam to seal. Place roll, seam side down, on a large greased baking sheet; shape into a ring, and pinch ends together to seal.

Cut dough at 1-inch intervals around ring, using a sharp knife or kitchen shears, cutting two-thirds of the way through. Gently turn each piece of dough on its side, slightly overlapping slices. Cover and let rise in a warm place (85°), free from drafts, 45 minutes or until doubled in bulk.

Bake at 375° for 20 minutes or until lightly browned. Remove to a wire rack.

Combine powdered sugar and orange juice, stirring well; drizzle over coffee cake. **Yield:** 1 coffee cake.

Cranberry Coffee Cake

Gumdrop Wreath Bread (photo on page 42)

1 package active dry yeast
¼ cup warm water (105° to 115°)
¾ cup milk
⅓ cup sugar
⅓ cup butter or margarine
1 teaspoon salt
3 large eggs, beaten
2 teaspoons grated lemon rind
5 to 5¼ cups all-purpose flour
¾ cup chopped gumdrops
½ cup chopped pecans
1½ cups sifted powdered sugar
2½ tablespoons milk
¼ teaspoon vanilla extract
Garnish: Gumdrop Roses

Combine yeast and warm water in a 1-cup liquid measuring cup; let stand 5 minutes.

Combine ¾ cup milk and next 3 ingredients in a saucepan; heat until butter melts, stirring occasionally. Cool to 105° to 115°.

Combine yeast mixture, milk mixture, eggs, and lemon rind; beat at medium speed of an electric mixer until blended. Add 2½ cups flour; beat about 2 minutes or until smooth. Stir in enough remaining flour to make a soft dough.

Turn dough out onto a floured surface, and knead until smooth and elastic (about 1 minute). Place in a well-greased bowl, turning to grease top. Cover and let rise in a warm place (85°), free from drafts, 45 minutes or until doubled in bulk.

Punch dough down; turn out onto a floured surface, and knead in gumdrops and pecans.

Invert a well-greased 5-inch metal mixing bowl in center of a large greased baking sheet. Shape dough into 1½-inch balls; place around bowl, forming a circle (stack some balls to add dimension). Cover and let rise in a warm place, free from drafts, 30 minutes or until doubled in bulk.

Bake at 375° for 15 to 18 minutes or until golden. Remove bowl; remove loaf to a wire rack.

Combine powdered sugar, 2½ tablespoons milk, and vanilla; drizzle over warm loaf. Garnish, if desired **Yield:** 1 loaf.

To MAKE GUMDROP ROSES: Set a gumdrop upright on a counter sprinkled with granulated sugar. Slice vertically into thirds. Flatten each third into an oval. Roll the smallest piece into a cone, pinching at narrow end for stem. Roll remaining pieces around cone, pressing upper edges outward and pinching at bottom. Slice another gumdrop to form leaves.

Raisin Bread

1 package active dry yeast
½ cup warm water (105° to 115°)
¼ cup sugar
1 cup butter or margarine, softened
6 large eggs
1 teaspoon salt
1 teaspoon grated orange rind
4½ cups all-purpose flour
1 cup golden raisins
1½ cups sifted powdered sugar
½ teaspoon rum flavoring
1 to 2 tablespoons water

Combine yeast and warm water in a 1-cup liquid measuring cup; let stand 5 minutes.

Combine yeast mixture, ¼ cup sugar, and next 4 ingredients in a large mixing bowl; add 2 cups flour, and beat at low speed of an electric mixer until blended. Beat 4 additional minutes. Stir in remaining 2½ cups flour and raisins.

Cover and let rise in a warm place (85°), free from drafts, 1½ hours or until doubled in bulk. Punch down; cover and chill at least 8 hours.

Turn out onto a floured surface; shape into an 18-inch rope. Shape into a ring; pinch ends together to seal. Place in a greased and floured 12-cup Bundt pan. Cover and let rise in a warm place, free from drafts, 1 hour or until doubled in bulk.

Bake at 350° for 45 minutes or until loaf sounds hollow when tapped. Remove from pan, and cool on a wire rack.

Combine powdered sugar, rum flavoring, and 1 to 2 tablespoons water; drizzle over loaf. **Yield:** 1 loaf.

Panettone

Panettone

2 packages active dry yeast
1 cup warm water (105° to 115°)
5 to 5½ cups all-purpose flour
½ cup sugar
½ cup butter or margarine, softened
3 large eggs
½ teaspoon salt
1 teaspoon ground nutmeg
½ cup chopped mixed candied fruit
½ cup raisins
1 tablespoon butter or margarine, melted
Honey

Cut a piece of aluminum foil long enough to fit around an 8-inch round cakepan, allowing a 1-inch overlap; fold lengthwise into thirds. Spray one side of aluminum foil with vegetable cooking spray; wrap foil around outside of cakepan, sprayed side against pan. Allow foil to extend 3 inches above rim of cakepan, forming a collar. Secure foil in place with freezer tape, and set cakepan aside.

Combine yeast and warm water in a 1-cup liquid measuring cup; let stand 5 minutes.

Place yeast mixture in a large mixing bowl. Add 2 cups flour, sugar, and next 4 ingredients; beat at medium speed of an electric mixer until smooth. Stir in candied fruit and raisins. Stir in enough remaining flour to make a soft dough.

Turn dough out onto a floured surface, and knead until smooth and elastic (about 5 minutes). Place in a well-greased bowl, turning to grease top. Cover and let rise in a warm place (85°), free from drafts, 1 hour or until doubled in bulk.

Punch dough down. Turn out onto a floured surface; knead 1 minute. Shape into a smooth ball; place in prepared pan. Brush top with 1 tablespoon melted butter. Gently cut a small X about ½ inch deep in top. Cover and let rise in a warm place, free from drafts, 1 hour.

Bake at 325° for 50 to 55 minutes or until loaf sounds hollow when tapped. (Cover with aluminum foil after 20 minutes to prevent excessive browning, if necessary.) Cool in pan on a wire rack 10 minutes; remove from pan, and cool on wire rack. Brush with honey. **Yield:** 1 loaf.

Hot Pepper-Cheese Bread

Tucked inside this buttery yeast bread is a melted pool of Monterey Jack cheese with jalapeño peppers.

1   cup milk
½   cup water
½   cup butter or margarine
4 to 4½   cups all-purpose flour
2   packages active dry yeast
1   tablespoon sugar
1   teaspoon salt
2   cups (8 ounces) shredded Monterey Jack cheese with jalapeño peppers
1   large egg, beaten
1   large egg, beaten
1   tablespoon milk

Combine first 3 ingredients in a saucepan; heat until butter melts, stirring occasionally. Cool to 120° to 130°.

Combine 2 cups flour, yeast, sugar, and salt in a large mixing bowl. Gradually add liquid mixture to flour mixture, beating at high speed of an electric mixer until blended. Beat 2 additional minutes at medium speed. Gradually stir in enough remaining flour to make a soft dough.

Turn dough out onto a floured surface, and knead until smooth and elastic (about 8 minutes). Place in a well-greased bowl, turning to grease top. Cover and let rise in a warm place (85°), free from drafts, 45 minutes or until doubled in bulk.

Punch dough down; cover and let rise in a warm place, free from drafts, 40 minutes or until doubled in bulk.

Punch dough down; remove one-fourth of dough, and set aside. Turn remaining dough out onto a lightly floured surface. Roll dough into a 20- to 22-inch circle. Place dough in a greased 9-inch cakepan, letting excess dough hang evenly over edges.

Roll reserved portion of dough into a 9-inch circle, and place on top of dough in pan.

Combine cheese and 1 egg, and spoon evenly onto dough. Fold and pleat excess dough over cheese mixture, gathering edges together in center and twisting to form a knob. Cover and let rise in a warm place, free from drafts, 15 minutes.

Bake at 375° for 40 minutes. (Cover with aluminum foil to prevent excessive browning, if necessary.) Combine 1 egg and 1 tablespoon milk; brush over bread. Bake 15 additional minutes. Cool in pan on a wire rack 10 minutes. Remove from pan, and cool on wire rack. **Yield:** 1 loaf.

Angel Biscuits

This biscuit dough will wait patiently in the refrigerator up to one week. (Punch the dough down before rolling and cutting.) There's no need to let the shaped dough rise in this recipe. The yeast here is used more for flavoring than for rising.

2   packages active dry yeast
2   tablespoons sugar
¼   cup warm water (105° to 115°)
5   cups self-rising flour
1   teaspoon baking soda
1   teaspoon salt
¾   cup shortening
2   cups buttermilk

Combine yeast and sugar in warm water in a 1-cup liquid measuring cup; let stand 5 minutes.

Combine flour, soda, and salt in a large mixing bowl; cut in shortening with pastry blender until mixture is crumbly. Add yeast mixture and buttermilk, stirring until dry ingredients are moistened.

Turn dough out onto a floured surface, and knead until smooth and elastic (about 8 to 10 minutes). Roll to ¼-inch thickness on a lightly floured surface. Cut with a 2½-inch biscuit cutter, and place ½ inch apart on lightly greased baking sheets. Bake at 450° for 10 to 12 minutes. **Yield:** 3½ dozen.

Jelly-Filled Doughnuts (photo on page 46)

1 package active dry yeast
¼ cup warm water (105° to 115°)
1 cup warm milk (105° to 115°)
4½ cups all-purpose flour
¾ cup plus 1 tablespoon sugar, divided
3 tablespoons butter or margarine, softened
1 large egg
¾ teaspoon salt
1½ teaspoons ground nutmeg
¼ cup currant jelly
Vegetable oil
Powdered sugar

Combine yeast and warm water in a 1-cup liquid measuring cup; let stand 5 minutes.

Combine yeast mixture, milk, 1½ cups flour, and 1 tablespoon sugar; beat at medium speed of an electric mixer until blended. Cover and let rise in a warm place (85°), free from drafts, 1 hour.

Beat butter and remaining ¾ cup sugar at medium speed until blended; add egg, salt, and nutmeg, and beat until smooth. Add butter mixture to yeast mixture; beat until blended. Gradually add remaining 3 cups flour, mixing well.

Place dough in a well-greased bowl, turning to grease top. Cover and let rise in a warm place, free from drafts, 1 hour or until doubled in bulk.

Punch dough down; turn out onto a floured surface, and knead 4 or 5 times.

Divide dough in half; keep 1 portion covered. Roll dough to ¼-inch thickness on a lightly floured surface. Cut into 24 rounds, using a 2½-inch round cutter. Place 12 rounds on a lightly greased baking sheet. Place ½ teaspoon jelly in center of each round. Brush edges of each jelly-topped round with water. Place remaining rounds over jelly-filled rounds; pinch edges to seal. Repeat procedure with remaining portion of dough. Cover and let rise in a warm place, free from drafts, 45 minutes or until doubled in bulk.

Pour oil to depth of 3 inches into a Dutch oven; heat to 375°. Cook doughnuts, 3 at a time, 1 minute on each side or until golden. Drain. Sprinkle with powdered sugar. **Yield:** 2 dozen.

Almond Twists (photo on page 46)

1 package active dry yeast
½ cup warm water (105° to 115°)
4½ cups all-purpose flour
¼ cup sugar
1 teaspoon salt
1 teaspoon grated orange rind
1 cup butter or margarine, softened
6 large eggs
1 (8-ounce) can almond paste
¾ cup firmly packed brown sugar
½ cup butter or margarine, softened
¼ cup chopped almonds, toasted
2 cups sifted powdered sugar
3 tablespoons milk

Combine yeast and warm water in a 1-cup liquid measuring cup; let stand 5 minutes.

Combine yeast mixture, 3 cups flour, ¼ cup sugar, and next 4 ingredients in a large mixing bowl; beat at low speed of an electric mixer until blended. Beat 4 additional minutes at medium speed. Add remaining 1½ cups flour; beat at low speed until blended. Cover and let rise in a warm place (85°), free from drafts, 1½ hours or until doubled in bulk. Cover and chill at least 8 hours.

Combine almond paste, brown sugar, ½ cup butter, and almonds; stir well, and set aside.

Punch dough down, and divide in half. Cover and chill 1 portion of dough. Roll remaining portion into a 16- x 10-inch rectangle on a floured surface. Spread half of almond paste mixture over dough. Fold dough lengthwise into thirds, forming a long rectangle. Cut into 16 (1-inch) strips. Twist each strip, and place on a lightly greased baking sheet. Repeat procedure with remaining dough and almond paste mixture.

Cover and let rise in a warm place, free from drafts, 1½ hours or until doubled in bulk.

Bake at 350° for 15 minutes or until lightly browned. Remove to wire racks.

Combine powdered sugar and milk; drizzle over warm rolls. **Yield:** 32 twists.

Brown Sugar Cinnamon Rolls

2 packages active dry yeast
1 cup warm water (105° to 115°)
½ cup butter or margarine, softened
½ cup shortening
¾ cup sugar
1 cup boiling water
2 large eggs, beaten
2 teaspoons salt
About 6 cups all-purpose flour
¼ cup butter or margarine, softened
½ cup firmly packed brown sugar
½ cup chopped walnuts
1 teaspoon ground cinnamon

Combine yeast and warm water in a 1-cup liquid measuring cup; let stand 5 minutes.

Beat ½ cup butter and shortening in a large mixing bowl at medium speed of an electric mixer until creamy; gradually add ¾ cup sugar and boiling water, beating well. Cool to 105° to 115°. Add yeast mixture, eggs, salt, and 2 cups flour; beat at low speed until smooth. Stir in enough remaining flour to make a soft dough.

Place in a well-greased bowl, turning to grease top. Cover and chill 8 hours.

Roll into a 24- x 18-inch rectangle on a lightly floured surface; spread ¼ cup butter evenly over dough. Combine brown sugar, walnuts, and cinnamon; sprinkle evenly over dough. Roll up, jellyroll fashion, starting at long side; pinch edges to seal. Cut roll into 1-inch slices; place slices, cut side down, in greased muffin pans.

Cover and let rise in a warm place (85°), free from drafts, 1 hour or until doubled in bulk.

Bake at 375° for 20 to 25 minutes. Remove from pans, and cool on wire racks. **Yield:** 2 dozen.

Overnight Potato Rolls

These rolls are a Test Kitchens' favorite because they're unusually light and can be made ahead. To make ahead, bake them for 3 to 5 minutes, and then wrap in aluminum foil, and freeze. To serve, let the rolls thaw, and bake at 425° for 5 minutes or until lightly browned.

1 package active dry yeast
½ cup warm water (105° to 115°)
1 cup milk
½ cup sugar
1 cup instant mashed potatoes (prepared
        without salt or fat)
⅔ cup butter-flavored shortening
1½ teaspoons salt
2 large eggs
5¾ to 6¼ cups all-purpose flour
Melted butter or margarine

Combine yeast and warm water in a 1-cup liquid measuring cup; let stand 5 minutes.

Combine milk and next 4 ingredients in a medium saucepan; cook, stirring constantly, until shortening melts. Cool to 105° to 115°.

Combine yeast mixture, milk mixture, and eggs in a large mixing bowl. Gradually add 3 cups flour, beating at medium speed of an electric mixer until smooth. Stir in enough remaining flour to make a soft dough.

Place in a well-greased bowl, turning to grease top; cover and chill 8 hours.

Punch dough down; turn out onto a floured surface, and knead 4 or 5 times. Roll dough to ½-inch thickness; cut with a 2½-inch round cutter.

Dip rolls in butter, and place 1 inch apart on lightly greased baking sheets. Cover and let rise in a warm place (85°), free from drafts, 2 hours.

Bake at 425° for 8 to 10 minutes or until lightly browned. **Yield:** 2½ dozen.

NOTE: To make cloverleaf rolls, shape dough into ¾-inch balls; place 3 balls in each well-greased muffin cup. Proceed as directed.

Herb-Buttered
Crescents

Herb-Buttered Crescents

Change the flavor of these tender, flaky crescents with a made-to-order herb butter. Experiment by using herbs like oregano and basil in place of chives and parsley.

2 packages active dry yeast
½ cup warm water (105° to 115°)
1 cup milk
½ cup sugar
½ cup sour cream
½ cup butter or margarine
2 large eggs, beaten
2 teaspoons salt
5½ to 6 cups all-purpose flour
Herb Butter

Combine yeast and warm water in a 1-cup liquid measuring cup; let stand 5 minutes.

Combine milk and next 3 ingredients in a saucepan; cook over low heat until butter melts, stirring occasionally. Cool to 105° to 115°.

Combine yeast mixture, milk mixture, eggs, salt, and 2 cups flour; beat at medium speed of an electric mixer 2 minutes. Stir in enough remaining flour to make a medium-stiff dough.

Place in a well-greased bowl, turning to grease top. Cover and chill 8 to 48 hours.

Turn out onto a floured surface; knead until smooth and elastic. Divide into 4 portions. Roll each into a 12-inch circle on a floured surface; spread with 2 tablespoons Herb Butter. Cut each circle into 12 wedges; roll each wedge, jellyroll fashion, starting at wide end.

Place rolls, point side down, 2 inches apart on greased baking sheets; curve into crescent shapes. Cover and let rise in a warm place (85°), free from drafts, 40 to 45 minutes or until doubled in bulk.

Bake at 375° for 10 to 15 minutes or until lightly browned. **Yield:** 4 dozen.

Herb Butter
½ cup butter or margarine, softened
2 tablespoons chopped fresh chives
1½ tablespoons minced fresh parsley
2 teaspoons lemon juice
⅛ teaspoon ground red pepper

Combine all ingredients. **Yield:** ½ cup.

Wheat-Sour Cream Rolls

Wheat-Sour Cream Rolls

2 packages active dry yeast
½ cup warm water (105° to 115°)
1 (8-ounce) carton sour cream
½ cup firmly packed brown sugar
½ cup butter or margarine
1 teaspoon salt
2 large eggs, beaten
2½ cups all-purpose flour
1⅓ cups whole wheat flour
3 tablespoons untoasted wheat germ
¼ teaspoon ground cardamom
¼ cup butter or margarine, melted

Combine yeast and warm water in a 1-cup liquid measuring cup; let stand 5 minutes.

Combine sour cream and next 3 ingredients in a heavy saucepan; cook over low heat until butter melts, stirring occasionally. Cool to 105° to 115°.

Combine yeast mixture, sour cream mixture, and eggs in a large bowl. Combine flours, wheat germ, and cardamom; gradually add to yeast mixture, stirring well. Cover and chill at least 8 hours.

Punch dough down; shape and bake into desired rolls.

VARIATIONS
CRESCENTS: Divide dough into 4 portions. Roll each portion into a 10-inch circle on a lightly floured surface, and brush with 1 tablespoon melted butter. Cut each circle into 12 wedges; roll each wedge, jellyroll fashion, starting at wide end. Place rolls, point side down, 2 inches apart on greased baking sheets; curve into crescent shapes. Cover and let rise in a warm place (85°), free from drafts, 45 minutes or until doubled in bulk. Bake at 375° for 10 minutes or until lightly browned. **Yield:** 4 dozen.

PAN ROLLS: Shape dough into 1½-inch balls. Place 16 balls ½ inch apart in two lightly greased 9-inch round cakepans. Cover and let rise in a warm place (85°), free from drafts, until doubled in bulk. Bake at 375° for 15 to 20 minutes or

until lightly browned. Brush with ¼ cup melted butter. **Yield:** 32 rolls.

CLOVERLEAF ROLLS: Shape dough into 1-inch balls; place 3 dough balls in each lightly greased muffin cup. Cover and let rise in a warm place (85°), free from drafts, until doubled in bulk. Bake at 375° for 10 to 12 minutes or until lightly browned. Brush with ¼ cup melted butter. **Yield:** 32 rolls.

Cheesy Pretzel Rolls

1 (16-ounce) package hot roll mix with yeast packet
½ cup (2 ounces) shredded sharp Cheddar cheese
1 cup hot water (120° to 130°)
2 tablespoons butter or margarine
1 large egg
1 large egg, lightly beaten
Kosher salt, sesame seeds, or poppy seeds (optional)

Combine hot roll mix with yeast packet and cheese in a large bowl; add hot water, butter, and 1 egg, stirring until blended.

Turn dough out onto a floured surface, and knead until smooth and elastic (about 5 minutes). Cover and let rest 5 minutes.

Cut dough into 24 pieces; roll each piece on a lightly floured surface into a 9-inch rope. Twist into a pretzel shape. Place on lightly greased baking sheets. Brush with beaten egg and, if desired, sprinkle with salt, sesame seeds, or poppy seeds.

Bake at 400° for 12 to 14 minutes or until golden. Serve warm. **Yield:** 2 dozen.

Cream-Filled
Chocolate Cake
(page 65)

Frosty Fixings

Cakes

*H*olidays demand spectacular cakes. Our showstopping collection includes Cream-Filled Chocolate Cake crowned with a supple chocolate ribbon and Chocolate-Raspberry Roulage atop a pool of almond-kissed raspberry sauce.

Chocolate-Raspberry
Roulage (page 72)

Chocolate-Caramel Cake

A dreamy caramel filling cuddles up to moist layers of chocolate cake, and then both are capped with a fluffy marshmallow frosting. A stylish drizzle of melted chocolate over the top and down the sides of the cake adds panache.

⅔ cup butter or margarine, softened
1½ cups sugar
½ cup firmly packed brown sugar
3 (1-ounce) squares unsweetened chocolate, melted
3 large eggs
2⅓ cups sifted cake flour
2 teaspoons baking soda
½ teaspoon salt
1⅓ cups buttermilk
⅓ cup water
1¼ teaspoons vanilla extract
Caramel Filling
½ cup chopped pecans
Fluffy Marshmallow Frosting
2 (1-ounce) squares unsweetened chocolate, melted
Shaved unsweetened chocolate

Beat butter in a large mixing bowl at medium speed of an electric mixer until creamy; gradually add sugars, beating well. Add 3 squares melted chocolate, and beat well. Add eggs, one at a time, beating after each addition.

Combine flour, soda, and salt; add to butter mixture alternately with buttermilk and water, beginning and ending with flour mixture. Mix at low speed after each addition until blended. Stir in vanilla. Pour batter into three greased and floured 9-inch round cakepans.

Bake at 350° for 25 to 30 minutes or until a wooden pick inserted in center comes out clean. Cool in pans on wire racks 10 minutes; remove from pans, and cool completely on wire racks.

Spread half of Caramel Filling on top of 1 cake layer; sprinkle with half of pecans. Carefully spread a ½-inch-thick layer of Fluffy Marshmallow Frosting over pecans; top with second cake layer. Spread with remaining filling; sprinkle with remaining pecans. Carefully spread a ½-inch-thick layer of frosting over pecans; top with remaining cake layer. Spread remaining frosting on top and sides of cake. Drizzle 2 squares melted chocolate around edges and down sides of cake. Sprinkle shaved chocolate on top of cake. **Yield:** one 3-layer cake.

Caramel Filling

1 cup firmly packed brown sugar
3 tablespoons all-purpose flour
1 cup evaporated milk
2 egg yolks, lightly beaten
2 tablespoons butter or margarine

Combine sugar and flour in a saucepan; gradually stir in milk. Cook over medium heat, stirring constantly, until mixture thickens and boils. Boil 1 minute, stirring constantly. Gradually stir about one-fourth of hot mixture into yolks; add to remaining hot mixture, stirring constantly. Return to a boil; boil 1 minute, stirring constantly. Remove from heat; add butter, stirring until butter melts. Cool. **Yield:** about 2½ cups.

Fluffy Marshmallow Frosting

2 egg whites
1½ cups sugar
⅓ cup water
1 tablespoon plus 2 teaspoons light corn syrup
16 large marshmallows, quartered

Combine first 4 ingredients in top of a large double boiler; beat at low speed of an electric mixer 1 minute or just until blended. Place mixture over boiling water; beat constantly at high speed 7 minutes. Transfer mixture to a large mixing bowl. Add marshmallows, and beat until spreading consistency. **Yield:** enough for one 3-layer cake.

Special
Chocolate Cake
(page 64)

Chocolate-Caramel Cake

Special Chocolate Cake

(photo on page 63)

2 (1-ounce) squares unsweetened chocolate
3 tablespoons water
¾ cup butter or margarine, softened
2¼ cups sugar
4 large eggs, separated
1 teaspoon vanilla extract
2¼ cups sifted cake flour
1 teaspoon cream of tartar
½ teaspoon baking soda
½ teaspoon salt
1 cup milk
Vanilla Cream Filling
Chocolate-Cream Cheese Frosting
¼ cup chopped almonds, toasted

Combine chocolate and water in a small saucepan; cook over low heat, stirring constantly, until chocolate melts. Remove from heat, and let cool slightly.

Beat butter in a large mixing bowl at medium speed of an electric mixer until creamy; gradually add sugar, beating well. Add egg yolks, one at a time, beating after each addition. Add cooled chocolate mixture and vanilla, beating until well blended.

Combine flour, cream of tartar, soda, and salt; add to butter mixture alternately with milk, beginning and ending with flour mixture. Mix at low speed after each addition until blended.

Beat egg whites at high speed until stiff peaks form; gently fold into batter. Pour batter evenly into three greased and floured 9-inch round cakepans.

Bake at 350° for 25 to 30 minutes or until a wooden pick inserted in center of cake layers comes out clean. Cool in pans on wire racks 10 minutes; remove from pans, and cool completely on wire racks.

Spread Vanilla Cream Filling between layers. Spread Chocolate-Cream Cheese Frosting on top and sides of cake. Sprinkle almonds on top of cake. Cover and chill 3 to 4 hours before serving. **Yield:** one 3-layer cake.

Vanilla Cream Filling

½ cup sugar
3 tablespoons all-purpose flour
⅛ teaspoon salt
1½ cups milk
2 large eggs, beaten
¼ cup chopped almonds, toasted
½ teaspoon vanilla extract

Combine sugar, flour, and salt in a heavy saucepan; gradually stir in milk. Cook over medium heat, stirring constantly, until mixture is smooth and thickened. Gradually stir about one-fourth of hot mixture into eggs; add to remaining hot mixture, stirring constantly. Bring to a boil; cook, stirring constantly, 2 to 3 minutes or until thickened. Remove from heat; stir in almonds and vanilla. Cover and chill 1 to 2 hours. **Yield:** enough for one 3-layer cake.

Chocolate-Cream Cheese Frosting

1 (8-ounce) package cream cheese, softened
¼ cup butter or margarine, softened
3 cups sifted powdered sugar, divided
3 (1-ounce) squares unsweetened chocolate, melted
1 tablespoon plus 1 teaspoon whipping cream
½ teaspoon vanilla extract
Dash of salt

Beat cream cheese and butter in a medium mixing bowl at medium speed of an electric mixer until creamy; add 1 cup powdered sugar and remaining 4 ingredients, beating well. Add remaining 2 cups sugar, and beat until spreading consistency. **Yield:** enough for one 3-layer cake.

Cream-Filled Chocolate Cake

(photo on page 60)

1 cup boiling water
¾ cup cocoa
2 tablespoons butter or margarine, softened
2 cups sugar
2 cups sifted cake flour
1 teaspoon baking soda
½ teaspoon baking powder
1 teaspoon salt
½ cup shortening
½ cup buttermilk
2 large eggs
1 teaspoon vanilla extract
Cream Filling
Chocolate Frosting
Chocolate Bow

Grease bottoms and sides of three 8-inch round cakepans; line with wax paper, and grease wax paper. Set aside.

Combine first 3 ingredients; set aside.

Combine sugar and next 4 ingredients in a large mixing bowl; add cocoa mixture and shortening, and beat at medium speed of an electric mixer until blended. Add buttermilk, eggs, and vanilla, and beat at medium speed 2 minutes.

Pour batter into prepared pans. Bake at 350° for 20 to 25 minutes or until a wooden pick inserted in center comes out clean. Cool in pans on wire racks 10 minutes; remove from pans, remove wax paper, and cool on wire racks.

Spread Cream Filling between cake layers. Spread Chocolate Frosting on top and sides of cake. Top cake with Chocolate Bow. **Yield:** one 3-layer cake.

Cream Filling

¼ cup milk
2 tablespoons all-purpose flour
¼ cup shortening
2 tablespoons butter or margarine, softened
2 teaspoons vanilla extract
⅛ teaspoon salt
2 cups sifted powdered sugar

Combine milk and flour in a small saucepan; cook over low heat, stirring constantly with a wire whisk, until mixture begins to thicken. Cover and chill at least 1 hour.

Beat shortening and butter in a medium mixing bowl at low speed of an electric mixer until creamy. Add chilled flour mixture, vanilla, and salt; beat until smooth. Gradually add powdered sugar; beat at high speed 4 to 5 minutes or until fluffy. **Yield:** 1¼ cups.

Chocolate Frosting

½ cup butter or margarine, softened
3 (1-ounce) squares unsweetened chocolate, melted
⅓ cup milk
2 teaspoons vanilla extract
1 (16-ounce) package powdered sugar, sifted

Beat butter and chocolate at low speed of an electric mixer until smooth. Add milk and vanilla, beating until blended. Gradually add powdered sugar; beat at high speed 5 minutes or until frosting is fluffy. **Yield:** 2½ cups.

Chocolate Bow

6 (1-ounce) squares semisweet chocolate
3½ tablespoons light corn syrup

Melt chocolate in a small saucepan over low heat; stir in corn syrup. Cover and chill 1 hour.

Knead mixture until consistency of dough. (Kneading with warm hands keeps chocolate soft; letting it stand on a cool surface hardens it.) Roll out onto a cool surface to ⅛-inch thickness. Using a fluted pastry wheel, cut into seven 8- to 10-inch strips (about ¼ inch wide). Place ends of 5 strips together to form loops. Turn a 9-inch round cakepan upside down; arrange loops to form a bow, and loosely attach remaining 2 strips for ribbon. Let stand 8 hours. Carefully remove pieces; arrange on top of cake. **Yield:** 1 bow.

NOTE: Chocolate Bow mixture can be kneaded until consistency of dough, and then wrapped and stored at room temperature up to 1 month.

Holiday Coconut Cake

⅓ cup butter, softened
⅓ cup shortening
1¾ cups sugar
3 cups sifted cake flour
3½ teaspoons baking powder
¾ teaspoon salt
1⅓ cups milk
2 teaspoons vanilla extract
4 egg whites
Lemon Filling
Fluffy Frosting
1 cup freshly grated coconut

Beat butter and shortening in a large mixing bowl at medium speed of an electric mixer until creamy; gradually add sugar, beating well.

Combine flour, baking powder, and salt; add to butter mixture alternately with milk, beginning and ending with flour mixture. Mix at low speed after each addition until blended. Stir in vanilla.

Beat egg whites at high speed until stiff peaks form; fold into batter. Pour batter into three greased and floured 9-inch round cakepans.

Bake at 350° for 25 minutes or until a wooden pick inserted in center comes out clean. Cool in pans on wire racks 10 minutes; remove from pans, and cool completely on wire racks.

Spread Lemon Filling between layers. Frost top and sides of cake with Fluffy Frosting, and sprinkle with coconut. **Yield:** one 3-layer cake.

Lemon Filling

1 cup plus 2 tablespoons sugar
¼ cup cornstarch
1 cup plus 2 tablespoons water
2 egg yolks, lightly beaten
3 tablespoons fresh lemon juice
1 tablespoon grated lemon rind
2 tablespoons butter

Combine sugar and cornstarch in a saucepan; gradually stir in water. Cook over medium heat, stirring constantly, until mixture thickens and boils. Boil 1 minute, stirring constantly. Slowly stir about one-fourth of hot mixture into yolks; add to remaining hot mixture. Return to a boil; boil, stirring constantly, 1 minute or until thickened. Remove from heat, and stir constantly until smooth. Add lemon juice, lemon rind, and butter, stirring until butter melts. Cool. **Yield:** about 2 cups.

Fluffy Frosting

1 cup sugar
⅓ cup water
¼ teaspoon cream of tartar
2 egg whites
½ teaspoon almond extract
½ teaspoon vanilla extract

Combine sugar, water, and cream of tartar in a heavy saucepan. Cook over medium heat, stirring constantly, until clear. Cook, without stirring, until mixture reaches soft ball stage or candy thermometer registers 240°. While syrup cooks, beat egg whites at high speed of an electric mixer until soft peaks form. Continue beating, adding 240° syrup in a heavy stream. Add flavorings; continue beating just until stiff peaks form and frosting is spreading consistency. **Yield:** enough for one 3-layer cake.

CRACKING A FRESH COCONUT

To get to the meat of a coconut, punch holes in the "eyes," and drain the juice. Use a hammer to crack the shell and break the coconut open. Then, pry the meat away from the shell with a knife or a clean screwdriver. Remove the brown skin from the meat, using a vegetable peeler. Shred the coconut with a grater or food processor.

Strawberry-Glazed
Christmas Cake

Strawberry-Glazed Christmas Cake

1   cup butter or margarine, softened
1   cup sugar
6   large eggs, separated
2   cups sifted cake flour
½   teaspoon baking powder
½   teaspoon salt
¾   cup sugar
3   cups whipping cream
2   tablespoons powdered sugar
1   teaspoon vanilla extract
1   (12-ounce) jar strawberry preserves,
        divided
1½   cups chopped pecans

Beat butter at medium speed of an electric mixer until creamy. Gradually add 1 cup sugar; beat well. Add egg yolks, one at a time, beating after each addition. Combine flour, baking powder, and salt; gradually add to butter mixture. Mix at low speed after each addition until blended.

Beat egg whites at high speed until foamy. Gradually add ¾ cup sugar, 1 tablespoon at a time, beating until stiff peaks form and sugar dissolves (2 to 4 minutes); fold into batter. Pour batter into three greased and floured 9-inch round cakepans.

Bake at 350° for 18 to 20 minutes or until a wooden pick inserted in center of cake layers comes out clean. Cool in pans on wire racks 10 minutes; remove from pans, and cool completely on wire racks.

Beat whipping cream until foamy; gradually add 2 tablespoons powdered sugar and vanilla, beating until soft peaks form.

Spread 1 cup sweetened whipped cream between each layer, and drizzle each with about ⅓ cup strawberry preserves. Spread top and sides with remaining sweetened whipped cream. Carefully pat pecans around sides.

Place remaining strawberry preserves in container of an electric blender; process until smooth, stopping once to scrape down sides. Drizzle pureed preserves on top of cake in lines about 1½ inches apart. Carefully pull a wooden pick through lines at 1-inch intervals. Store in refrigerator. **Yield:** one 3-layer cake.

Sweet Potato Cake with Fresh Coconut Filling

1½ cups sugar
1 cup vegetable oil
4 large eggs, separated
2¾ cups sifted cake flour
1 tablespoon baking powder
¼ teaspoon salt
2 teaspoons ground cinnamon
1 teaspoon ground ginger
½ teaspoon ground cloves
1½ cups peeled, shredded sweet potato
¼ cup hot water
½ cup chopped walnuts
Fresh Coconut Filling
Garnish: orange rind bow

Combine sugar and oil; beat at medium speed of an electric mixer 2 minutes. Add egg yolks, one at a time, beating after each addition.

Combine flour and next 5 ingredients; add flour mixture, sweet potato, hot water, and walnuts to sugar mixture. Mix at low speed until blended.

Beat egg whites at high speed until stiff peaks form; fold into batter. Pour batter into three greased and floured 8-inch round cakepans.

Bake at 350° for 30 to 35 minutes or until a wooden pick inserted in center comes out clean. Cool in pans on wire racks 10 minutes; remove from pans, and cool completely on wire racks.

Spread filling between layers and on top of cake. Garnish, if desired. Cover and chill 3 to 4 hours before serving. **Yield:** one 3-layer cake.

Fresh Coconut Filling

½ cup sugar
¼ cup cornstarch
¼ teaspoon salt
2 cups milk
2 large eggs, beaten
1 cup freshly grated coconut
1 teaspoon vanilla extract

Combine first 3 ingredients in a heavy saucepan; gradually stir in milk. Cook over medium heat, stirring constantly, until thickened and bubbly. Gradually stir about one-fourth of hot mixture into eggs; add to remaining hot mixture, stirring constantly. Return to a boil; boil, stirring constantly, 1 minute or until thickened. Remove from heat; stir in coconut and vanilla. Cool; cover and chill 1 to 2 hours. **Yield:** enough for one 3-layer cake.

Sweet Potato Cake with
Fresh Coconut Filling

Rich Fruitcake

1 (15-ounce) package golden raisins
¼ pound currants
½ cup dark rum
1 (16-ounce) package candied yellow pineapple, chopped
1 (8-ounce) package candied red cherries, halved
1 (4-ounce) package candied citron, finely chopped
1 cup chopped almonds
1 cup chopped pecans
2 ounces candied lemon peel, finely chopped
2 ounces candied orange peel, finely chopped
2 cups all-purpose flour, divided
½ teaspoon baking soda
½ teaspoon ground mace
½ teaspoon ground cinnamon
½ cup butter, softened
1 cup sugar
1 cup firmly packed brown sugar
5 large eggs
1 tablespoon milk
1 teaspoon almond extract
½ cup dark rum

Draw a circle with a 10-inch diameter on a piece of brown paper, using a tube pan as a guide. (Do not use recycled paper.) Cut out circle; set tube pan insert in center, and draw around inside tube. Cut out smaller circle. Heavily grease and flour 10-inch tube pan; insert paper, and grease paper. Set aside.

Combine first 3 ingredients in a small bowl; cover and let stand at room temperature 8 hours.

Combine raisin mixture, pineapple, and next 6 ingredients in a large bowl; sprinkle with ½ cup flour, and stir gently to coat. Set aside.

Combine remaining 1½ cups flour, soda, mace, and cinnamon; set aside.

Beat butter at medium speed of an electric mixer until creamy; gradually add sugars, beating well. Add eggs, one at a time, beating after each addition. Stir in milk and almond extract. Add flour mixture, and beat until blended. Pour batter over candied fruit mixture, and stir until fruit is evenly coated. Pour batter into prepared pan.

Bake at 275° for 3 hours and 15 minutes or until a wooden pick inserted in center comes out clean. Cool in pan on a wire rack 30 minutes; remove from pan, and cool completely on wire rack. Wrap cake in cheesecloth, and pour ½ cup rum evenly over top. Seal in an airtight container; let stand at least two weeks before serving. Yield: one 10-inch cake.

Cranberry Cake

3 cups all-purpose flour
1 teaspoon baking soda
¼ teaspoon salt
2 cups sugar
1 cup vegetable oil
1 cup buttermilk
2 large eggs
2 cups fresh or frozen cranberries, thawed
1 cup chopped pecans
1 cup whole pitted dates, chopped
1 tablespoon grated orange rind
¼ cup sugar
¼ cup fresh orange juice

Combine first 3 ingredients; set aside.

Combine 2 cups sugar and next 3 ingredients in a large mixing bowl; beat at medium speed of an electric mixer until blended. Add flour mixture; mix at low speed just until blended. Stir in cranberries and next 3 ingredients. Pour batter into a greased and floured 12-cup Bundt pan.

Bake at 350° for 1 hour and 5 minutes or until a wooden pick inserted in center comes out clean. Cool in pan on a wire rack 10 minutes; remove from pan, and place on a serving plate.

Combine ¼ cup sugar and orange juice in a small saucepan; bring to a boil, stirring constantly until sugar dissolves. Immediately brush warm orange juice mixture over warm cake. Cool completely. Yield: one 10-inch cake.

Applesauce-Spice Pound Cake

Applesauce laces this pound cake with homespun goodness. A blend of brown sugar, cinnamon, nutmeg, and cloves adds sweet spice, while a handful of raisins and pecans imparts rustic charm.

1 cup butter or margarine, softened
1½ cups firmly packed brown sugar
1½ cups sugar
5 large eggs
1½ cups applesauce
2 teaspoons baking soda
3 cups all-purpose flour, divided
1 teaspoon ground cinnamon
1 teaspoon ground nutmeg
½ teaspoon ground cloves
½ teaspoon ground allspice
1½ cups raisins
1 cup chopped pecans

Beat butter in a large mixing bowl at medium speed of an electric mixer about 2 minutes or until soft and creamy. Gradually add sugars, beating at medium speed 5 to 7 minutes. Add eggs, one at a time, beating just until yellow disappears.

Combine applesauce and soda; set aside.

Combine 2¾ cups flour and spices; add to butter mixture alternately with applesauce mixture, beginning and ending with flour mixture. Mix at low speed just until blended after each addition.

Combine remaining ¼ cup flour, raisins, and pecans; fold into batter. Pour batter into a greased and floured 12-cup Bundt pan.

Bake at 325° for 1 hour and 15 to 20 minutes or until a wooden pick inserted in center comes out clean. Cool in pan on a wire rack 10 to 15 minutes; remove from pan, and cool completely on wire rack. **Yield:** one 10-inch cake.

Gingerbread Pound Cake

1 cup butter or margarine, softened
1 cup sugar
5 large eggs
2 cups all-purpose flour
½ teaspoon baking soda
1 teaspoon ground ginger
1 teaspoon ground cinnamon
1 teaspoon ground cloves
1 cup molasses
½ cup sour cream
Sifted powdered sugar
Lemon Sauce (optional)

Beat butter in a mixing bowl at medium speed of an electric mixer about 2 minutes or until soft and creamy; gradually add 1 cup sugar, beating at medium speed 5 to 7 minutes. Add eggs, one at a time, beating just until yellow disappears.

Combine flour, soda, and spices. Combine molasses and sour cream. Add flour mixture to butter mixture alternately with molasses mixture, beginning and ending with flour mixture. Mix at low speed just until blended after each addition. Pour into a greased and floured 12-cup Bundt pan.

Bake at 325° for 1 hour or until a wooden pick inserted in center comes out clean. Cool in pan on a wire rack 10 to 15 minutes; remove from pan. Cool completely on wire rack. Sprinkle with powdered sugar. Serve with warm Lemon Sauce, if desired. **Yield:** one 10-inch cake.

Lemon Sauce

1 cup water
½ cup sugar
2 tablespoons cornstarch
1 tablespoon butter or margarine
2 teaspoons grated lemon rind
⅓ cup fresh lemon juice

Combine first 3 ingredients in a saucepan; cook over medium heat, stirring constantly, until mixture is smooth and thickened. Stir in butter, lemon rind, and lemon juice, and cook until heated. **Yield:** 1⅔ cups.

Two-Tone
Pound Cake

Two-Tone Pound Cake

No need to teeter between chocolate and vanilla when choosing a cake. This duo-tone tempter binds both into one marbled creation.

1¼ cups butter or margarine, softened
2½ cups sugar
5 large eggs
2⅔ cups all-purpose flour
1¼ teaspoons baking powder
½ teaspoon salt
1 cup milk
2 teaspoons vanilla extract
¼ cup cocoa
Sifted powdered sugar

Beat butter in a large mixing bowl at medium speed of an electric mixer about 2 minutes or until soft and creamy. Gradually add 2½ cups sugar, beating at medium speed 5 to 7 minutes. Add eggs, one at a time, beating just until yellow disappears.

Combine flour, baking powder, and salt; add to butter mixture alternately with milk, beginning and ending with flour mixture. Mix at low speed after each addition just until blended. Stir in vanilla.

Remove 2 cups batter, and stir in cocoa. Spoon one-third of remaining batter into a greased and floured 13-cup Bundt pan; top with half of chocolate batter. Repeat layers, ending with plain batter. Gently swirl batter with a knife to create a marbled effect.

Bake at 325° for 1 hour and 5 minutes or until a wooden pick inserted in center comes out clean. Cool in pan on a wire rack 10 to 15 minutes; remove from pan, and cool completely on wire rack. Sprinkle with powdered sugar. **Yield:** one 10-inch cake.

Chocolate-Raspberry Roulage

(photo on page 60)

½ cup sifted cake flour
3 tablespoons cocoa
¾ teaspoon baking powder
3 large eggs, separated
½ cup sugar, divided
2 tablespoons milk
⅛ teaspoon salt
1 to 2 tablespoons powdered sugar
1 cup whipping cream
3 tablespoons powdered sugar
1 teaspoon vanilla extract
1 (10-ounce) jar seedless red raspberry jam,
    divided
Powdered sugar
Raspberry Sauce
Garnishes: sifted powdered sugar, fresh
    mint sprigs, fresh raspberries,
    whipped cream

Grease bottom and sides of a 15- x 10- x 1-inch jellyroll pan; line with wax paper, and grease wax paper. Set aside.

Combine flour, cocoa, and baking powder, and set aside.

Beat egg yolks in a large mixing bowl at high speed of an electric mixer until foamy. Gradually add ¼ cup sugar, beating until thick and pale (about 5 minutes). Stir in milk; add flour mixture, stirring until blended.

Beat egg whites and salt at high speed until foamy; gradually add remaining ¼ cup sugar, 1 tablespoon at a time, beating until soft peaks form. Fold into batter. Spread evenly into prepared pan.

Bake at 375° for 10 to 12 minutes or until cake springs back when lightly touched in center. Sift 1 to 2 tablespoons powdered sugar in a 15- x 10-inch rectangle on a cloth towel or work surface. When cake is done, immediately loosen from sides of pan with a knife, and turn out onto sugar. Peel off wax paper. Starting at narrow side, roll up cake and towel together, and place, seam side down, on a wire rack to cool completely.

Beat whipping cream until foamy; gradually add 3 tablespoons powdered sugar and vanilla, beating until soft peaks form. Unroll cake. Reserve 2 tablespoons raspberry jam for Raspberry Sauce; spread remaining jam over cake. Carefully spread whipped cream mixture over jam.

Reroll cake, without towel, and place, seam side down, on a serving plate. Sprinkle with additional powdered sugar. To serve, place each cake slice on top of 2½ tablespoons Raspberry Sauce. Garnish, if desired. **Yield:** 8 servings.

Raspberry Sauce

2 (10-ounce) packages frozen whole red
    raspberries, thawed
2 tablespoons cornstarch
2 tablespoons reserved seedless red
    raspberry jam
½ teaspoon almond extract

Place raspberries in container of an electric blender; process until smooth, stopping once to scrape down sides. Pour raspberry puree through a wire-mesh strainer into a bowl, discarding seeds; set aside.

Combine cornstarch, jam, and almond extract in a small saucepan; cook over medium heat, stirring constantly, until cornstarch dissolves. Stir in raspberry puree; cook over medium heat, stirring constantly, until mixture thickens and boils. Boil 1 minute, stirring constantly. Remove from heat. Cover and chill. **Yield:** 1¼ cups.

White Chocolate Roulage

A heavenly white chocolate filling nestles within a delicate cake spiral. Crown the cake with a halo of white chocolate curls.

4 large eggs, separated
¾ cup sugar, divided
1 tablespoon vegetable oil
1 teaspoon vanilla extract
⅔ cup sifted cake flour
1 teaspoon baking powder
¼ teaspoon salt
1 to 2 tablespoons powdered sugar
White Chocolate Cream Filling
Garnish: white chocolate curls

Oil a 15- x 10- x 1-inch jellyroll pan with vegetable oil; line with wax paper, and lightly oil and flour wax paper. Set aside.

Beat egg yolks in a large mixing bowl at high speed of an electric mixer until foamy. Gradually add ¼ cup sugar, beating until mixture is thick and pale (about 5 minutes). Stir in 1 tablespoon vegetable oil and vanilla; set aside.

Beat egg whites at high speed until foamy; gradually add remaining ½ cup sugar, 1 tablespoon at a time, beating until stiff peaks form and sugar dissolves (2 to 4 minutes). Fold into yolk mixture. Combine flour, baking powder, and salt; gradually fold into egg mixture. Spread batter evenly into prepared pan.

Bake at 350° for 8 to 10 minutes or until cake springs back when lightly touched in center. Sift powdered sugar in a 15- x 10-inch rectangle on a cloth towel or work surface. When cake is done, immediately loosen from sides of pan with a knife, and turn out onto sugar. Peel off wax paper. Starting at narrow side, roll up cake and towel together, and place, seam side down, on a wire rack to cool completely.

Unroll cake. Spread cake with half of White Chocolate Cream Filling, and carefully reroll cake, without towel. Place, seam side down, on a serving plate; spread remaining filling on top and sides of cake. Garnish, if desired. **Yield:** 8 servings.

White Chocolate Cream Filling

1½ teaspoons unflavored gelatin
3 tablespoons cold water
1 (6-ounce) package white baking bar, grated*
1¼ cups whipping cream
1 teaspoon vanilla extract

Sprinkle gelatin over water in a small saucepan; let stand 1 minute. Cook over low heat, stirring until gelatin dissolves, about 2 minutes. Add grated baking bar, and cook, stirring constantly, until baking bar melts; cool slightly.

Combine whipping cream and gelatin mixture in a medium mixing bowl; beat at medium speed of an electric mixer until thickened. Stir in vanilla. Cover and chill. **Yield:** 3 cups.

* For the white baking bar, we used Nestlé Premier White Baking Bar.

White Chocolate Roulage

Turtle Cheesecake (photo on cover)

2 cups chocolate wafer crumbs
¼ cup sugar
⅓ cup butter, melted
3 (8-ounce) packages cream cheese, softened
1¼ cups sugar
4 large eggs
1 (8-ounce) carton sour cream
1 tablespoon vanilla extract
¼ cup butter
1 cup (6 ounces) semisweet chocolate
　　morsels
1 (12-ounce) jar caramel topping*
1 cup chopped pecans

Combine first 3 ingredients; stir well. Firmly press mixture on bottom and 1 inch up sides of a lightly greased 9-inch springform pan. Bake at 325° for 10 minutes. Cool in pan on a wire rack.

Beat cream cheese at medium speed of an electric mixer until creamy; gradually add 1¼ cups sugar, beating well. Add eggs, one at a time, beating well after each addition and scraping sides and bottom as needed. Stir in sour cream and vanilla. Pour batter into prepared crust. Bake at 325° for 1 hour and 5 minutes. (Center will not be completely set.) Turn oven off; partially open oven door. Leave cheesecake in oven 1 hour. Remove to a wire rack to cool completely. Cover and chill at least 8 hours. Carefully remove sides of pan; transfer cheesecake to serving plate.

Melt ¼ cup butter in small heavy saucepan; add chocolate morsels. Stir over low heat just until chocolate melts and mixture blends. Spread warm chocolate mixture over cheesecake; chill 15 minutes.

Combine caramel topping and pecans in a small saucepan. Bring to a boil, stirring constantly, over medium heat; boil 2 minutes. Remove from heat, and cool 5 minutes. Spread over chocolate; cool completely. Serve immediately, or cover and chill. **Yield:** one 9-inch cheesecake.

* For caramel topping, we used Smuckers' brand.

Chocolate-Candy Cheesecake

1 (9-ounce) package chocolate wafer cookies,
　　crushed
¼ cup sugar
¼ cup butter or margarine, melted
2 (2.07-ounce) chocolate-coated caramel-
　　peanut nougat bars, coarsely chopped*
2 (8-ounce) packages cream cheese, softened
½ cup sugar
2 large eggs
¾ cup (4.5 ounces) semisweet chocolate
　　morsels, melted
1 teaspoon vanilla extract
1 cup whipping cream, whipped

Combine first 3 ingredients; firmly press mixture in bottom and 1½ inches up sides of an ungreased 9-inch springform pan. Sprinkle chopped candy bars evenly over bottom; set aside.

Beat cream cheese in a large mixing bowl at high speed of an electric mixer until creamy; gradually add ½ cup sugar, beating well. Add eggs, one at a time, beating after each addition. Stir in melted chocolate morsels and vanilla; beat mixture until blended. Spoon batter over candy bar layer in pan.

Bake at 350° for 30 minutes. Gently run a knife around edge of pan to release sides. Cool to room temperature in pan on a wire rack. Cover and chill at least 8 hours.

To serve, carefully remove sides of springform pan. Pipe or dollop whipped cream on top of cheesecake. **Yield:** 12 servings.

* For chocolate-coated caramel-peanut nougat bars, we used Snickers candy bars.

Peanut Brittle
Cheesecake

Peanut Brittle Cheesecake

1½ cups graham cracker crumbs
⅓ cup finely crushed peanut brittle
⅓ cup butter or margarine, melted
3 (8-ounce) packages cream cheese, softened
1 cup sugar
5 large eggs
1 tablespoon grated orange rind
1 teaspoon vanilla extract
½ cup whipping cream, whipped
2 tablespoons finely crushed peanut brittle
1 maraschino cherry with stem

Combine cracker crumbs, ⅓ cup brittle, and butter; firmly press mixture in bottom and up sides of a buttered 8-inch springform pan. Set aside.

Beat cream cheese in a large mixing bowl at medium speed of an electric mixer until creamy; gradually add sugar, beating well after each addition. Add eggs, one at a time, beating after each addition. Stir in orange rind and vanilla. Pour batter into prepared pan.

Bake at 300° for 1 hour and 15 to 20 minutes. Gently run a knife around edge of pan to release sides. Cool to room temperature in pan on a wire rack. Cover and chill 8 hours.

To serve, carefully remove sides of springform pan. Pipe whipped cream around edge of cheesecake, and sprinkle with 2 tablespoons peanut brittle. Top with cherry. **Yield:** 10 servings.

Festive Fruit Pie with
Cinnamon Sauce (page 78)

Festive Trimmings

Pies and Pastries

Winter fruits, nuts, spices, and traditional flavors of the season inspire this potpourri of pies. Whether you're looking for something nestled under a crown of flaky crust, a pillow of whipped cream, or a golden halo of meringue, you'll find a hearty slice of these holiday pies is heavenly.

Apple Pie with Walnut Topping

Petite pearly beads of tapioca plus whipping cream thicken the sweet juices emerging from the apple slices as they bake. A crunchy topping of walnuts, brown sugar, and graham cracker crumbs adds mahogany magic.

4   cups peeled, thinly sliced cooking apple
¾   cup whipping cream
1   tablespoon lemon juice
¾   cup sugar
1½ tablespoons quick-cooking tapioca
⅛   teaspoon salt
½   teaspoon ground cinnamon
¼   teaspoon ground nutmeg
1   unbaked 9-inch pastry shell
Walnut Crumb Topping

   Combine first 3 ingredients in a bowl; let stand at room temperature 15 minutes.
   Combine sugar and next 4 ingredients; add to apple mixture, stirring gently to combine. Spoon into pastry shell.
   Bake at 425° for 10 minutes; sprinkle with Walnut Crumb Topping. Reduce oven temperature to 350°, and bake 30 additional minutes. Cool on a wire rack. Serve with ice cream. **Yield:** one 9-inch pie.

Walnut Crumb Topping
½   cup firmly packed brown sugar
½   cup graham cracker crumbs
¼   cup all-purpose flour
¼   cup chopped walnuts
½   teaspoon ground cinnamon
¼   cup butter or margarine, melted

   Combine first 5 ingredients; add butter, and stir well. **Yield:** about 1¼ cups.

Festive Fruit Pie with Cinnamon Sauce
(photo on page 76)

Pastry for double-crust 9-inch pie
3   cooking apples, peeled and sliced (about 1 pound)
2   pears, peeled and sliced (about ¾ pound)
1   cup fresh cranberries
1   tablespoon lemon juice
½   cup sugar
½   cup firmly packed brown sugar
½   cup all-purpose flour
½   teaspoon ground cinnamon
¼   teaspoon ground nutmeg
2   tablespoons butter or margarine
Cinnamon Sauce

   Roll half of pastry to ⅛-inch thickness on a lightly floured surface. Place in a 9-inch deep-dish pieplate; set aside.
   Combine apple and next 3 ingredients; toss gently. Combine sugars and next 3 ingredients; add to apple mixture, and toss gently. Spoon into pastry shell, and dot with butter.
   Roll out remaining pastry to ⅛-inch thickness on a lightly floured surface, and place over apple mixture. Trim off excess pastry along edges. Fold edges under, and crimp. Cut several slits in top pastry to allow steam to escape. Bake at 375° for 45 minutes. Cool on a wire rack. Serve with warm Cinnamon Sauce. **Yield:** one 9-inch pie.

Cinnamon Sauce
1   cup water
½   cup sugar
2   tablespoons cornstarch
1   teaspoon ground cinnamon
½   teaspoon ground nutmeg
3   tablespoons lemon juice
1   tablespoon butter or margarine

   Combine all ingredients in a small saucepan. Cook over medium heat, stirring constantly, until mixture comes to a boil. Boil 1 minute, stirring constantly. **Yield:** 1 cup.

Festive Cranberry Pie

A twist of the wrist while weaving the pastry strips into a lattice atop this pie creates a stunning visual treat.

¾ cup sugar
¾ cup light corn syrup
½ cup water
2 tablespoons grated orange rind
1 tablespoon cornstarch
3 cups fresh cranberries
½ cup raisins
½ cup coarsely chopped pecans
2 tablespoons butter or margarine
Pastry for double-crust 9-inch pie
2 teaspoons sugar

Combine first 5 ingredients in a large saucepan; bring to a boil, stirring constantly. Stir in cranberries, raisins, and pecans. Cover, reduce heat, and cook 7 to 10 minutes or until cranberry skins pop. Remove from heat, and stir in butter; cool completely without stirring.

Roll half of pastry to ⅛-inch thickness on a lightly floured surface; place in a 9-inch pieplate. Spoon filling into pastry shell.

Roll remaining pastry to ¼-inch thickness; cut into 1-inch strips. Weave strips over filling in a lattice fashion, twisting each strip while weaving. Press ends of strips into rim of crust; flute edge. Sprinkle pie with 2 teaspoons sugar. Bake at 400° for 40 minutes. Cool on a wire rack. **Yield:** one 9-inch pie.

Pumpkin Pie with Spiced Cream Sauce

This holiday favorite boasts a double dusting of pumpkin pie spice—first in the filling, and then in the accompanying cream sauce.

½ (15-ounce) package refrigerated piecrusts
1 (16-ounce) can pumpkin
1 (14-ounce) can sweetened condensed milk
2 large eggs, beaten
¼ cup firmly packed brown sugar
1 teaspoon pumpkin pie spice
¼ teaspoon vanilla extract
Spiced Cream Sauce (optional)

Fit piecrust into a 9-inch pieplate according to package directions; fold edges under, and crimp. Prick bottom and sides of piecrust generously with a fork. Bake at 450° for 8 minutes; cool.

Combine pumpkin and next 5 ingredients, stirring well; pour into prepared piecrust. Bake at 350° for 50 to 55 minutes or until a knife inserted in center comes out clean. Cool on a wire rack. Serve with Spiced Cream Sauce, if desired. **Yield:** one 9-inch pie.

Spiced Cream Sauce
½ cup sour cream
2 tablespoons brown sugar
¼ teaspoon pumpkin pie spice
¼ cup whipping cream

Combine first 3 ingredients in a small bowl, stirring well. Let stand at room temperature 3 minutes. Gradually add whipping cream, stirring until blended. Cover and chill. **Yield:** ¾ cup.

Black Forest Pie

¾ cup sugar
⅓ cup cocoa
2 tablespoons all-purpose flour
⅓ cup milk
¼ cup butter or margarine
2 large eggs, beaten
1 (21-ounce) can cherry pie filling, divided
1 unbaked 9-inch pastry shell
1 cup whipping cream
1½ tablespoons powdered sugar
Garnish: grated semisweet chocolate

Combine first 3 ingredients in a small saucepan; stir well. Gradually stir in milk. Add butter; cook over medium heat, stirring constantly, until mixture thickens. Remove from heat. Gradually stir about one-fourth of hot mixture into eggs; add to remaining hot mixture, stirring constantly. Cook over medium-low heat 2 minutes, stirring constantly. Remove from heat. Stir in half of pie filling.

Spoon into pastry shell. Bake at 350° for 35 minutes or until center is set, but still shiny. Cool on a wire rack. Cover and chill 1 hour.

Black Forest Pie

Combine whipping cream and powdered sugar; beat until soft peaks form. Pipe whipped cream around edge of pie. Garnish, if desired. Spoon remaining pie filling into center of pie. Chill. **Yield:** one 9-inch pie.

Chocolate-Eggnog Layer Pie

Dressed in holiday style, this black bottom pie is accessorized with eggnog.

1 envelope unflavored gelatin
½ cup cold water
⅓ cup sugar
2 tablespoons cornstarch
¼ teaspoon salt
2 cups refrigerated eggnog
1½ (1-ounce) squares unsweetened chocolate, melted
1 teaspoon vanilla extract
1 baked 9-inch pastry shell
1 teaspoon rum extract
2 cups whipping cream, divided
¼ cup sifted powdered sugar
Garnish: semisweet chocolate curls

Sprinkle gelatin over cold water; stir and let stand 1 minute.

Combine ⅓ cup sugar, cornstarch, and salt in a saucepan. Gradually stir in eggnog; cook over medium heat, stirring constantly, until mixture is thickened. Remove from heat; add gelatin mixture, and stir until gelatin dissolves.

Divide filling in half; set half of filling aside, and cool. Stir melted chocolate and vanilla into remaining half of filling. Pour into pastry shell. Cover and chill until set.

Stir rum extract into reserved filling. Beat 1 cup whipping cream until soft peaks form; fold into filling mixture. Spoon over chocolate layer; cover and chill.

Beat remaining 1 cup whipping cream until foamy; gradually add powdered sugar, beating until soft peaks form. Spread over pie. Garnish, if desired. **Yield:** one 9-inch pie.

Coconut Cream Pie

Coconut Cream Pie

Dainty flakes of coconut lace this velvety vanilla custard pie.

¾ cup sugar
3 tablespoons cornstarch
¼ teaspoon salt
2 cups milk
3 large eggs, separated
1 (3½-ounce) can flaked coconut, divided
2 tablespoons butter or margarine
1 teaspoon vanilla extract
1 baked 9-inch pastry shell
¼ teaspoon cream of tartar
½ teaspoon vanilla extract
¼ cup plus 2 tablespoons sugar

Combine ¾ cup sugar, cornstarch, and salt in a medium saucepan; gradually stir in milk. Cook over medium heat, stirring constantly, until mixture is thickened.

Beat egg yolks until thick and pale. Gradually stir about one-fourth of hot mixture into yolks; add to remaining hot mixture, stirring constantly. Cook over medium heat 5 minutes, stirring constantly. Remove from heat; stir in 1 cup coconut, butter, and 1 teaspoon vanilla. Spoon into pastry shell.

Beat egg whites, cream of tartar, and ½ teaspoon vanilla at high speed of an electric mixer until foamy. Gradually add ¼ cup plus 2 tablespoons sugar, 1 tablespoon at a time, beating mixture until stiff peaks form and sugar dissolves (2 to 4 minutes).

Spread meringue over hot filling, sealing to edge of pastry.

Sprinkle with remaining coconut. Bake at 325° for 25 to 28 minutes or until golden. Cool on a wire rack. Chill 1 hour before serving. **Yield:** one 9-inch pie.

Macadamia Pie

Buttery bits of macadamia nuts punctuate this pleasing pie. A warm rum syrup cascades over each ample wedge.

1 cup dark corn syrup
⅔ cup sugar
3 large eggs, lightly beaten
1 cup finely chopped macadamia nuts
¼ cup butter or margarine, melted
1 unbaked 9-inch pastry shell
Rum Syrup

Combine first 3 ingredients in a medium bowl; stir in macadamia nuts and butter. Pour into pastry shell. Bake at 350° for 30 to 35 minutes or until set. Cool on a wire rack. Serve with warm Rum Syrup. **Yield:** one 9-inch pie.

Rum Syrup
2 tablespoons butter or margarine
½ cup firmly packed brown sugar
¼ cup dark corn syrup
2 tablespoons light rum
1 teaspoon vanilla extract

Melt butter in a saucepan over medium heat; stir in brown sugar and corn syrup. Cook, stirring constantly, until sugar dissolves and mixture comes to a boil. Remove from heat; stir in rum and vanilla. **Yield:** ⅔ cup.

Southern Pecan Pie

1 cup sugar
1 cup light corn syrup
½ cup butter or margarine
4 large eggs, beaten
1 teaspoon vanilla extract
¼ teaspoon salt
1 unbaked 9-inch pastry shell
1 cup pecan halves

Combine first 3 ingredients in a saucepan; cook over low heat, stirring constantly, until butter melts and sugar dissolves. Cool.
Add eggs, vanilla, and salt; stir well. Pour into pastry shell; top with pecan halves. Bake at 325° for 50 to 55 minutes. Cool on a wire rack. **Yield:** one 9-inch pie.

Caramel-Pecan Pie

A rich rivulet of caramel topping flows through a mound of chopped pecans beneath this pie's cream cheese filling.

1 cup coarsely chopped pecans
1 unbaked 9-inch pastry shell
¼ cup caramel topping
2 (3-ounce) packages cream cheese, softened
½ cup sugar
1 teaspoon vanilla extract
3 large eggs
Garnishes: pecan halves, caramel topping

Place 1 cup chopped pecans in bottom of pastry shell; drizzle with ¼ cup caramel topping. Set aside.
Combine cream cheese, sugar, and vanilla in a medium mixing bowl; beat at medium speed of an electric mixer until blended. Add eggs, one at a time, beating after each addition. Pour over pecans in pastry shell.
Bake at 325° for 45 minutes. Cool on a wire rack. Cover and chill. Garnish, if desired. **Yield:** one 9-inch pie.

Walnut Fudge Pie

A luxurious fudge sauce languishes over coffee ice cream on thick slices of chunky, chocolatey pie.

½ cup firmly packed brown sugar
¼ cup all-purpose flour
¼ cup butter or margarine, melted
1 teaspoon vanilla extract
3 large eggs, lightly beaten
2 cups (12 ounces) semisweet chocolate
        morsels, melted
1½ cups walnut halves
½ (15-ounce) package refrigerated piecrusts
Coffee ice cream
Heavenly Fudge Sauce (optional)

Combine first 5 ingredients in a large bowl, stirring until blended. Stir in melted chocolate and walnuts.

Fit piecrust into a 9-inch pieplate according to package directions. Fold edges under, and flute. Spoon filling into piecrust.

Bake at 375° for 30 minutes. Cool on a wire rack. Serve with coffee ice cream and warm Heavenly Fudge Sauce, if desired. **Yield:** one 9-inch pie.

Heavenly Fudge Sauce
2 cups (12 ounces) semisweet chocolate
        morsels
1 tablespoon butter or margarine
½ cup whipping cream
¼ cup strongly brewed coffee

Combine chocolate morsels and butter in a heavy saucepan. Cook over low heat until chocolate and butter melt, stirring often. Gradually whisk in whipping cream; cook, stirring constantly, 2 to 3 minutes or until smooth. Remove from heat; stir in coffee. **Yield:** 2 cups.

Walnut Fudge Pie

Banana Pudding Tarts

Banana Pudding Tarts

2 small bananas, sliced
10 baked 3-inch tart shells
1 (8-ounce) carton sour cream
1 cup milk
1 (3.4-ounce) package vanilla instant
    pudding mix
Garnishes: banana slices, whipped cream,
    maraschino cherries with stems

    Place 5 or 6 banana slices in each tart shell; set aside.

    Combine sour cream and milk in a medium mixing bowl; stir well. Add pudding mix, and beat at medium speed of an electric mixer 1 minute or until thickened. Spoon evenly over banana slices in tart shells. Garnish, if desired. **Yield:** 10 (3-inch) tarts.

Pecan Tarts

¾ cup firmly packed brown sugar
⅔ cup chopped pecans
1 tablespoon butter or margarine, melted
1 egg, lightly beaten
1 teaspoon vanilla extract
Cream Cheese Shells

    Combine all ingredients except Cream Cheese Shells in a medium bowl; stir until blended. Spoon filling evenly into shells. Bake at 350° for 17 minutes. **Yield:** 2 dozen (1¾-inch) tarts.

Cream Cheese Shells
½ cup butter or margarine, softened
1 (3-ounce) package cream cheese, softened
1 cup all-purpose flour

    Beat butter and cream cheese at medium speed of an electric mixer until creamy. Add flour, beating until blended. Cover and chill 1 hour.

    Shape dough into 24 balls. Place balls in greased miniature (1¾-inch) muffin pans, pressing dough on bottom and up sides to form shells. Bake at 350° for 15 minutes. **Yield:** 2 dozen.

Latticed Cranberry Tart

4 cups fresh cranberries
2 cups sugar
¾ cup water
4 egg yolks, beaten
2½ tablespoons all-purpose flour
Dash of salt
½ cup chopped pecans
2 tablespoons butter or margarine
½ teaspoon almond extract
Pastry
1 egg yolk, beaten
1 teaspoon water

Combine first 3 ingredients in a medium saucepan; cook over medium heat 5 to 7 minutes or until cranberry skins pop. Cool slightly.

Combine 4 egg yolks, flour, and salt. Gradually stir about one-fourth of cranberry mixture into yolk mixture; add to remaining cranberry mixture, stirring constantly. Cook over medium heat 1 minute or until thickened, stirring often. Remove from heat; add pecans, butter, and almond extract, stirring until butter melts.

Roll half of pastry to ⅛-inch thickness on a floured surface. Place in a 12- x 8- x 1-inch tart pan. Pour cranberry mixture into tart shell.

Roll remaining pastry to ⅛-inch thickness on a floured surface. Cut with a fluted pastry wheel into thin strips. Arrange strips over tart in a diagonal lattice design. Roll rolling pin over pastry on pan to trim excess pastry from edges. Combine 1 egg yolk and 1 teaspoon water; brush pastry with yolk mixture. Bake at 400° for 30 to 35 minutes or until browned. **Yield:** one 12-inch tart.

Pastry
2 cups all-purpose flour
2 tablespoons sugar
¾ teaspoon salt
⅔ cup plus 2 tablespoons shortening
4 to 6 tablespoons cold water

Combine flour, sugar, and salt; cut in shortening with pastry blender until flour mixture is crumbly. Sprinkle cold water (1 tablespoon at a time) evenly over surface; stir with a fork until dry ingredients are moistened. Shape into a ball; cover and chill 30 minutes. **Yield:** enough for one 12-inch tart.

Winter Fruit Crisp

3 cooking apples, unpeeled and sliced
    (about 1½ pounds)
2 cups fresh cranberries
1 (8-ounce) can unsweetened crushed
    pineapple, undrained
½ cup sugar
1 cup firmly packed brown sugar
¼ cup all-purpose flour
½ cup butter or margarine, softened
1 cup regular oats, uncooked
1 cup chopped pecans
Sweetened whipped cream

Layer first 3 ingredients in a lightly greased 13- x 9- x 2-inch baking dish; sprinkle with ½ cup sugar, and set aside.

Combine brown sugar and flour; cut in butter with pastry blender until mixture is crumbly. Stir in oats and pecans. Sprinkle over fruit. Bake, uncovered, at 375° for 30 minutes. Serve warm with whipped cream. **Yield:** 8 servings.

NOTE: To prepare this crisp the day before, sprinkle the pecan mixture over the fruit; cover and chill 8 hours. Let stand at room temperature 30 minutes. Uncover and bake at 375° for 30 minutes.

Christmas Fruitcake
Cookies (page 92)

German Chocolate
Fudge (page 104)

Eggnog Crescents
(page 92)

Visions of Sugarplums

Cookies and Candies

Our smorgasbord of sweet indulgences will delight young and old alike. You'll be able to keep your cookie jar and candy dish well stocked with this variety of doable and delectable confections.

Date-Nut Pinwheel Cookies

This splendid cookie dough makes three spiral rolls. Bake one right away, freeze one for last-minute baking, and share one with a friend.

1 (10-ounce) package chopped dates
½ cup sugar
1 cup hot water
1 cup very finely chopped walnuts
1 cup butter or margarine, softened
2 cups firmly packed brown sugar
2 large eggs
3½ cups all-purpose flour
½ teaspoon baking soda
½ teaspoon salt
½ teaspoon cream of tartar
1 teaspoon vanilla extract

Combine first 3 ingredients in a medium saucepan; cook over medium heat, stirring constantly, 8 minutes or until thickened. Remove from heat, and stir in walnuts; set aside to cool.

Beat butter in a large mixing bowl at medium speed of an electric mixer until creamy; gradually add brown sugar, beating well. Add eggs, beating until blended.

Combine flour and next 3 ingredients; gradually add to butter mixture, beating until blended. Stir in vanilla. Cover and chill 15 minutes.

Divide dough into thirds. Roll each portion into a 12-inch square on wax paper; spread each with one-third of date mixture to within ½ inch of edges. Lifting up edge of wax paper, gently peel off dough, and roll up, jellyroll fashion. Wrap rolls; chill at least 8 hours.

Cut rolls into ¼-inch slices, and place 2 inches apart on greased cookie sheets.

Bake at 350° for 8 to 10 minutes. Transfer to wire racks to cool. **Yield:** 9 dozen.

NOTE: If you don't want to wait for the cookie dough to chill 8 hours, wrap the rolls in wax paper, and freeze 2 hours. Let stand at room temperature 15 minutes before cutting.

Ribbon Cookies

Bands of cherry and chocolate cookie dough color these cookies in festive fashion.

1 cup butter or margarine, softened
1½ cups sugar
1 large egg
1 teaspoon vanilla extract
¼ teaspoon almond extract
2½ cups all-purpose flour
1½ teaspoons baking powder
½ teaspoon salt
½ cup finely chopped candied red cherries, divided
¼ cup chopped almonds
1 (1-ounce) square unsweetened chocolate, melted

Line bottom and sides of a 9- x 5- x 3-inch loafpan with plastic wrap; set aside.

Beat butter in a large mixing bowl at medium speed of an electric mixer until creamy; gradually add sugar, beating well. Add egg and flavorings, beating well.

Combine flour, baking powder, and salt; gradually add to butter mixture, beating until blended. (Dough will be stiff.)

Divide dough into thirds. Stir half of cherries into one-third of dough; press into prepared pan.

Stir almonds and melted chocolate into one-third of dough; press over dough in pan.

Stir remaining half of cherries into remaining one-third of dough; press over doughs in pan. Cover and chill at least 8 hours.

Invert pan, and remove dough; remove plastic wrap. Cut dough lengthwise into thirds. Cut each section of dough crosswise into ¼-inch slices. Place 1 inch apart on ungreased cookie sheets.

Bake at 350° for 10 to 12 minutes. Transfer to wire racks to cool. **Yield:** about 7 dozen.

Ribbon
Cookies

Date-Nut
Pinwheel Cookies

Christmas Bell
Cookies

Christmas Bell Cookies

Ring in the season with a batch of these clever cookies. Maraschino cherries serve as the jingle bell clappers.

2/3 cup butter or margarine, softened
3/4 cup sugar
1 large egg
1 teaspoon grated orange rind
1 teaspoon vanilla extract
2 cups all-purpose flour
1½ teaspoons baking powder
30 maraschino cherries, halved

Beat butter in a large mixing bowl at medium speed of an electric mixer until creamy; gradually add sugar, beating well. Add egg, orange rind, and vanilla, beating until blended.

Combine flour and baking powder; gradually add to butter mixture, beating until blended. Cover and chill 30 minutes.

Shape dough into 2 (8-inch) rolls. Wrap rolls; chill at least 8 hours.

Cut rolls into ¼-inch slices, and place 1 inch apart on ungreased cookie sheets. Place a cherry half on bottom half of each slice; fold in opposite sides, slightly overlapping, to partially cover each cherry half.

Bake at 350° for 10 to 12 minutes. Transfer to wire racks to cool. **Yield:** 5 dozen.

Christmas Fruitcake Cookies

(photo on page 88)

1 cup butter or margarine, softened
1½ cups sugar
2 large eggs
2½ cups all-purpose flour
1 teaspoon baking soda
½ teaspoon salt
1 teaspoon ground cinnamon
3 cups chopped pecans
1 (10-ounce) package chopped dates
1 (8-ounce) package candied yellow
    pineapple, chopped
1 (8-ounce) package candied red cherries,
    quartered

Beat butter at medium speed of an electric mixer until creamy; gradually add sugar, beating well. Add eggs, beating until blended.

Combine flour and next 3 ingredients; gradually add to butter mixture, beating until blended. Stir in pecans and remaining ingredients.

Drop dough by heaping teaspoonfuls onto lightly greased cookie sheets.

Bake at 375° for 10 minutes or until browned. Transfer to wire racks to cool. **Yield:** 6½ dozen.

Black-Eyed Susans

Semisweet chocolate morsels comprise the soft brown centers of these cheery faux flowers.

½ cup butter or margarine, softened
½ cup sugar
½ cup firmly packed brown sugar
1 cup peanut butter
1 large egg
1½ tablespoons warm water
1 teaspoon vanilla extract
1½ cups all-purpose flour
½ teaspoon baking soda
½ teaspoon salt
½ cup (3 ounces) semisweet chocolate
    morsels

Beat butter in a large mixing bowl at medium speed of an electric mixer until creamy; gradually add sugars, beating well. Add peanut butter and next 3 ingredients, beating until blended.

Combine flour, soda, and salt; add to peanut butter mixture, beating until blended.

Use a cookie gun with a flower-shaped disc, and shape dough into 1-inch cookies following manufacturer's instructions. Place 1 inch apart on lightly greased cookie sheets. Place a chocolate morsel in center of each cookie.

Bake at 350° for 8 minutes or until lightly browned. Transfer to wire racks to cool. **Yield:** about 10 dozen.

Eggnog Crescents (photo on page 88)

1 cup butter or margarine, softened
½ cup sifted powdered sugar
2 cups all-purpose flour
1 cup ground almonds
¼ teaspoon salt
¼ to ½ teaspoon rum extract
Rum Glaze
Ground nutmeg

Beat butter in a large mixing bowl at medium speed of an electric mixer until creamy; gradually add powdered sugar, beating until light and fluffy.

Combine flour, almonds, and salt; add to butter mixture, beating just until blended. Stir in rum extract.

Shape into 1-inch balls; shape each into a crescent. Place 1 inch apart on ungreased cookie sheets.

Bake at 325° for 12 to 15 minutes. Transfer to wire racks to cool. Drizzle with Rum Glaze. Sprinkle with nutmeg. **Yield:** 3½ dozen.

Rum Glaze
¾ cup sifted powdered sugar
1 tablespoon milk
⅛ teaspoon rum extract

Combine all ingredients in a small bowl, stirring until smooth. **Yield:** about ⅓ cup.

Date-Filled Cookies

1 cup shortening
½ cup sugar
½ cup firmly packed brown sugar
1 large egg
3 tablespoons milk
1 teaspoon vanilla extract
3 cups all-purpose flour
½ teaspoon baking soda
½ teaspoon salt
1 cup chopped pitted dates
¼ cup sugar
¼ cup water
Pinch of salt
1 tablespoon lemon juice

Beat shortening in a large mixing bowl at medium speed of an electric mixer until creamy; gradually add ½ cup sugar and ½ cup brown sugar, beating well. Add egg, milk, and vanilla, beating until blended.

Combine flour, soda, and ½ teaspoon salt; gradually add to shortening mixture, beating until blended.

Use a cookie gun with a flower-shaped disc, and shape dough into 2-inch cookies following manufacturer's instructions.

Place 1 inch apart on lightly greased cookie sheets. Use a small paring knife to remove center circle from half of cookies.

Bake at 375° for 10 to 12 minutes. Transfer to wire racks to cool.

Combine dates and next 3 ingredients in a small saucepan; bring to a boil. Cover, reduce heat, and simmer 5 minutes, stirring occasionally. Stir in lemon juice; cool.

Turn half of cookies with centers upside down; spread 1 teaspoon date mixture over each cookie. Top with cookies without centers. **Yield:** 3 dozen.

Date-Filled
Cookies

Lucky
Stars

Lucky Stars

A cluster of nutty maple filling peeks from the points of these star-shaped cookies and flavors them a lot like pecan pie.

¼ cup butter or margarine, softened
¼ cup sugar
1 large egg
1 teaspoon vanilla extract
1⅓ cups all-purpose flour
1½ teaspoons baking powder
⅛ teaspoon salt
Nut Filling

Beat butter in a large mixing bowl at medium speed of an electric mixer until creamy; gradually add sugar, beating well. Add egg and vanilla, beating until blended.

Combine flour, baking powder, and salt, stirring well. Add flour mixture to butter mixture, beating until blended.

Roll dough to ⅛-inch thickness on a lightly floured surface. Cut with a 2½-inch star-shaped cookie cutter, and place 1 inch apart on ungreased cookie sheets.

Place about 1 teaspoon Nut Filling in center of each cookie. Gently bring points of each star to the center; pinch points together to stand upright, allowing filling to show through sides.

Bake at 350° for 10 minutes or until lightly browned. Cool on cookie sheets 1 minute. Transfer to wire racks to cool. **Yield:** 4 dozen.

Nut Filling

1¼ cups finely chopped pecans or walnuts
⅓ cup sugar
2 tablespoons water
1 tablespoon butter or margarine, melted
⅛ teaspoon salt
⅛ teaspoon maple flavoring

Combine all ingredients in a small bowl, stirring well. **Yield:** 1¼ cups.

Chocolate Biscotti

Baking these cookies not once, but twice, makes them extra crisp and two times as nice for dunking into coffee or cocoa.

4 (1-ounce) squares unsweetened chocolate
½ cup butter or margarine
½ teaspoon vanilla extract
3 large eggs
1¼ cups sugar
3 cups all-purpose flour
½ teaspoon baking powder
1 cup walnuts or hazelnuts, chopped
1 egg white, lightly beaten

Combine chocolate and butter in a heavy saucepan; cook over low heat, stirring constantly, until chocolate and butter melt. Remove from heat, and stir in vanilla. Set aside to cool.

Beat eggs in a large mixing bowl at medium speed of an electric mixer until foamy; gradually add sugar, beating until thick and pale (about 5 minutes). Add chocolate mixture, stirring until blended.

Combine flour and baking powder; add to chocolate mixture, stirring until blended. Stir in walnuts.

Shape dough into a 13-inch log, using floured hands. Place on a lightly greased cookie sheet. Lightly brush with egg white.

Bake at 350° for 45 minutes. Transfer to a wire rack to cool.

Cut log crosswise into 24 (½-inch-thick) slices, using a serrated knife; place 1 inch apart on ungreased cookie sheets.

Bake at 350° for 10 minutes on each side. Transfer to wire racks to cool. **Yield:** 2 dozen.

Cocoa Surprise Cookies

We'll let you in on the surprise—a crème de menthe thin wafer hides inside each chocolate cookie.

1 cup butter or margarine, softened
⅔ cup sugar
1⅔ cups all-purpose flour
¼ cup cocoa
1 cup finely chopped pecans
½ teaspoon vanilla extract
½ teaspoon mint flavoring
36 crème de menthe thins (about 6 ounces)*
1 cup sifted powdered sugar
1½ tablespoons milk
2 or 3 drops of green liquid food coloring

Beat butter in a large mixing bowl at medium speed of an electric mixer until creamy; gradually add ⅔ cup sugar, beating well. Add flour and cocoa, beating until blended. Stir in pecans and flavorings. Cover and chill 2 hours.

Shape dough into 36 balls. Shape each ball into an oval shape around a crème de menthe thin. Place 2 inches apart on ungreased cookie sheets, and chill 30 minutes.

Bake at 375° for 12 minutes. Cool on cookie sheets 1 minute. Transfer to wire racks to cool.

Combine powdered sugar and milk, stirring until smooth; stir in food coloring. Place in a zip-top plastic bag. Using scissors, snip a tiny hole in one corner of bag; drizzle over cookies. **Yield:** 3 dozen.

* For crème de menthe thins, we used Andes brand.

Jam Kolaches

These buttery bundles reveal a dab of jam in their centers. Use your favorite fruit flavor to make this recipe your own.

½ cup butter or margarine, softened
1 (3-ounce) package cream cheese, softened
1¼ cups all-purpose flour
About 2 tablespoons strawberry jam
¼ cup sifted powdered sugar

Beat butter and cream cheese in a large mixing bowl at medium speed of an electric mixer until creamy; add flour, beating until blended.

Roll dough to ⅛-inch thickness on a floured surface; cut with a 2-inch round cookie cutter, and place 1 inch apart on greased cookie sheets.

Spoon ¼ teaspoon jam in center of cookies; fold in opposite sides, slightly overlapping edges.

Bake at 375° for 15 minutes. Transfer to wire racks to cool. Sprinkle with powdered sugar. **Yield:** about 2 dozen.

Cherry Delights

1 cup butter or margarine, softened
½ cup sugar
½ cup light corn syrup
2 large eggs, separated
2½ cups all-purpose flour
2 cups finely chopped pecans
24 candied cherries, halved

Beat butter at medium speed of an electric mixer until creamy; gradually add sugar, beating until light and fluffy. Add syrup and yolks, beating well. Add flour, beating until blended. Chill.

Beat egg whites at high speed until foamy. Shape dough into 1-inch balls; dip balls in egg white, and roll in pecans to coat. Place 1½ inches apart on greased cookie sheets. Press a cherry half, cut side down, in center of each ball.

Bake at 325° for 20 minutes. Transfer to wire racks to cool. **Yield:** 4 dozen.

Ginger Cookies

¾ cup shortening
1 cup sugar
1 large egg
¼ cup molasses
2 cups all-purpose flour
2 teaspoons baking soda
½ teaspoon salt
1 tablespoon ground ginger
1 teaspoon ground cinnamon
⅓ cup sugar

Beat shortening in a large mixing bowl at medium speed of an electric mixer until creamy; gradually add 1 cup sugar, beating well. Add egg and molasses, beating until blended.

Combine flour and next 4 ingredients; add to shortening mixture, beating until blended.

Shape into 1-inch balls; roll in ⅓ cup sugar. Place 2 inches apart on ungreased cookie sheets.

Bake at 350° for 8 to 10 minutes. Cool on cookie sheets 5 minutes. Transfer to wire racks to cool. **Yield:** 7 dozen.

Holiday Peppermint Puffs

⅔ cup butter-flavored shortening
¼ cup sugar
¼ cup firmly packed brown sugar
1 large egg
1½ cups all-purpose flour
½ teaspoon baking powder
½ teaspoon salt
½ cup crushed hard peppermint candy

Beat shortening at medium speed of an electric mixer until creamy; gradually add sugars, beating well. Add egg, beating until blended.

Combine flour, baking powder, and salt; add to shortening mixture, beating well. Stir in candy.

Shape dough into 1-inch balls; place 2 inches apart on greased cookie sheets. Bake at 350° for 12 minutes. Transfer to wire racks to cool. **Yield:** 3½ dozen.

Lemon Bonbons

These golden goodies make a light and lemony addition to your cookie tray.

1 cup butter, softened
⅓ cup sifted powdered sugar
1¼ cups all-purpose flour
¾ cup cornstarch
½ cup finely chopped pecans
All-purpose flour
1½ cups sifted powdered sugar
1½ teaspoons butter, softened
1½ tablespoons lemon juice

Beat 1 cup butter at medium speed of an electric mixer until creamy; gradually add ⅓ cup powdered sugar, beating until light and fluffy. Add 1¼ cups flour and cornstarch, beating until mixture is blended. Cover and chill 1 hour.

Shape dough into 1-inch balls; roll balls in pecans to coat.

Place 2 inches apart on ungreased cookie sheets; flatten to ¼-inch thickness with a flat-bottomed glass dipped in flour.

Bake at 350° for 12 to 14 minutes. Transfer to wire racks to cool.

Combine 1½ cups powdered sugar, 1½ teaspoons butter, and lemon juice; stir until smooth. Spread on top of cookies. **Yield:** 2½ dozen.

Shortbread Cookies

⅓ cup butter
¼ cup sugar
2 teaspoons cognac, brandy, or vanilla
      extract
1 cup all-purpose flour
⅛ teaspoon salt
Sugar

Position knife blade in food processor bowl; add butter and ¼ cup sugar, and pulse 5 times.

Sprinkle mixture with cognac; add flour and salt. Process 30 seconds or until blended.

Shape dough into ¾-inch balls; place 2 inches apart on ungreased cookie sheets. Flatten to ¼-inch thickness with a cookie stamp or flat-bottomed glass dipped in sugar.

Bake at 350° for 12 minutes or until edges begin to brown. Transfer to wire racks to cool. **Yield:** 2 dozen.

Date-Nut Balls

1 (10-ounce) package chopped dates
¾ cup sugar
½ cup butter or margarine
2½ cups crisp rice cereal*
1 cup chopped pecans
Flaked coconut or powdered sugar

Combine first 3 ingredients in a saucepan. Bring mixture to a boil; cook 3 minutes, stirring constantly.

Stir in cereal and pecans; cool to touch. Shape mixture into 1-inch balls; roll balls in coconut. **Yield:** 4½ dozen.

* For crisp rice cereal, we used Kellogg's Rice Krispies.

Royal Rum Balls

Royal Rum Balls

These resplendent rum balls are fit for a king. The longer they sit, the grander the taste.

2 cups gingersnap crumbs
2 cups chocolate wafer crumbs
1½ cups sifted powdered sugar
1 cup flaked coconut
1 cup ground pecans, toasted
⅓ cup pitted dates, chopped
⅓ cup dark rum
3 tablespoons light corn syrup
2 tablespoons butter or margarine, melted
1 teaspoon vanilla extract
Sifted powdered sugar or gingersnap crumbs

Position knife blade in food processor bowl; add first 6 ingredients. Process until blended, stopping once to scrape down sides.

Add rum and next 3 ingredients to mixture in processor bowl. Process until mixture holds together, stopping once to scrape down sides.

Shape into 1¼-inch balls; roll balls twice in additional powdered sugar or gingersnap crumbs. Yield: 3 dozen.

NOTE: If you make Royal Rum Balls ahead, reroll balls in powdered sugar or gingersnap crumbs before serving to freshen the coating, if desired.

Chunks-of-Chocolate Brownies

1 cup plus 2 tablespoons all-purpose flour
½ teaspoon baking powder
¼ teaspoon salt
1¾ cups sugar
¾ cup cocoa
½ cup shortening
4 large eggs, beaten
2¼ teaspoons vanilla extract
¾ cup chopped pecans
1 cup semisweet chocolate mega morsels
Chocolate Frosting

Combine first 5 ingredients in a large bowl; stir well. Cut in shortening with pastry blender until mixture is crumbly.

Add eggs and vanilla, stirring until blended. Stir in pecans and mega morsels.

Spoon batter into a greased and floured 13- x 9- x 2-inch pan.

Bake at 350° for 25 minutes. Cool in pan on a wire rack. Spread with Chocolate Frosting. Cut into squares. Yield: 3 dozen.

Chocolate Frosting

1 cup sugar
¼ cup plus 1 tablespoon butter or margarine
¼ cup milk
1 cup semisweet chocolate mega morsels
½ teaspoon vanilla extract

Combine first 3 ingredients in a saucepan. Bring to a boil; reduce heat, and cook 2 minutes, stirring constantly. Remove from heat; add mega morsels and vanilla, stirring until morsels melt. Yield: 1½ cups.

Cranberry Bars

Whole-berry cranberry sauce makes a quick and easy filling for these wholesome oatmeal bar cookies.

1½ cups all-purpose flour
1½ cups quick-cooking oats, uncooked
¾ cup firmly packed brown sugar
¼ teaspoon baking soda
1 teaspoon grated lemon rind
¾ cup butter or margarine
1 (16-ounce) can whole-berry cranberry
     sauce
¼ cup chopped walnuts or pecans

Combine first 5 ingredients in a large bowl; cut in butter with pastry blender until mixture is crumbly. Set 1 cup flour mixture aside. Press remaining flour mixture in bottom of an ungreased 13- x 9- x 2-inch pan. Bake at 350° for 20 minutes.

Remove from oven; stir cranberry sauce, and spread over warm crust. Combine reserved flour mixture and walnuts; sprinkle over cranberry sauce, and press gently.

Return to oven, and bake 25 to 30 additional minutes. Cool in pan on a wire rack. Cut into bars. **Yield:** 2 dozen.

Chocolate Chip Toffee Grahams

11 whole graham crackers (4½ x 2¼
      inches), broken into squares
1 cup sugar
1 cup butter or margarine
½ cup finely chopped pecans
1 teaspoon ground cinnamon
1 cup semisweet chocolate mini-morsels

Arrange graham cracker squares in a single layer in an ungreased 15- x 10- x 1-inch jellyroll pan. Set aside.

Combine sugar and butter in a heavy saucepan. Bring to a boil over medium heat, stirring constantly. Boil 2 minutes, stirring constantly. Remove from heat; stir in pecans and cinnamon. Pour evenly over graham crackers, spreading to edges of pan.

Bake at 350° for 10 to 12 minutes. Sprinkle with mini-morsels. Cool in pan on a wire rack. Separate cookies, and place on wax paper-lined cookie sheets. Chill until firm. Store between layers of wax paper in an airtight container in refrigerator. **Yield:** 22 cookies.

Coconut Bars

A citrus glaze caps these chewy coconut, brown sugar, and pecan treats.

¾ cup butter or margarine, softened
¾ cup sifted powdered sugar
1½ cups all-purpose flour
2 large eggs
1 cup firmly packed brown sugar
½ cup chopped pecans
½ cup flaked coconut
2 tablespoons all-purpose flour
½ teaspoon baking powder
½ teaspoon salt
½ teaspoon vanilla extract
1 cup sifted powdered sugar
3 tablespoons orange juice
2 tablespoons butter or margarine, melted
1 teaspoon lemon juice

Beat ¾ cup butter in a large mixing bowl at medium speed of an electric mixer until creamy; gradually add ¾ cup powdered sugar, beating well. Add 1½ cups flour, beating until blended.

Press dough into an ungreased 13- x 9- x 2-inch pan. Bake at 350° for 12 minutes. Remove from oven. Combine eggs and next 7 ingredients; pour evenly over crust. Return to oven, and bake 20 additional minutes.

Combine 1 cup powdered sugar and remaining 3 ingredients; pour over warm cookies. Cool in pan on a wire rack. Cut into bars. **Yield:** 3 dozen.

Caramel-Pecan Chews

2 cups sugar
1 cup light corn syrup
3 cups whipping cream, divided
3 cups chopped pecans
1 teaspoon vanilla extract

Combine sugar, syrup, and 1 cup whipping cream in a heavy Dutch oven; cook over medium heat until mixture reaches thread stage or candy thermometer registers 230°, stirring often.

Stir in 1 cup whipping cream; cook, stirring constantly, until mixture reaches thread stage or candy thermometer registers 230°. Stir in remaining 1 cup whipping cream; cook, stirring constantly, until mixture reaches soft ball stage or candy thermometer registers 240°. Remove from heat; add pecans and vanilla. Pour into a buttered 13- x 9- x 2-inch pan; cool. Cut into 1½- x ½-inch strips; roll each in a 5- x 4-inch piece of wax paper, twisting ends. **Yield:** 12 dozen.

Hard-Crack Christmas Candy

1 tablespoon powdered sugar
2 cups sugar
½ cup water
½ cup light corn syrup
½ teaspoon strawberry flavoring
10 drops of red liquid food coloring

Sift 1 tablespoon powdered sugar in a 15- x 10- x 1-inch jellyroll pan; set aside.

Combine 2 cups sugar, water, and corn syrup in a heavy saucepan. Cook over medium heat until mixture reaches hard crack stage or candy thermometer registers 300°, stirring occasionally. Stir in strawberry flavoring and food coloring.

Pour into prepared pan; cool. Break into pieces. **Yield:** 1 pound.

Peanutty Clusters (page 105)

Caramel-Pecan Chews

Hard-Crack Christmas Candy

Peanut Butter
Squares
(page 105)

Raspberry
Divinity

Peppermint-
Chocolate Truffles

Raspberry Divinity

Raspberry gelatin and almonds make these rosy candies flush with flavor.

3 cups sugar
¾ cup water
¾ cup light corn syrup
¼ teaspoon salt
2 egg whites
1 (3-ounce) package raspberry-flavored gelatin
1 cup chopped slivered almonds, toasted

Combine first 4 ingredients in a heavy 3-quart saucepan; cook over low heat, stirring constantly, until sugar dissolves. Cover and cook over medium heat 2 to 3 minutes to wash down sugar crystals from sides of saucepan. Uncover and cook over medium heat, without stirring, until mixture reaches hard ball stage or candy thermometer registers 258°. Remove saucepan from heat.

Beat egg whites in a large mixing bowl at high speed of an electric mixer until foamy. Add raspberry-flavored gelatin, and beat until stiff peaks form. Gradually pour hot syrup mixture in a thin stream over egg whites, beating constantly at high speed until mixture holds its shape (3 to 4 minutes). Quickly stir in almonds.

Drop mixture by rounded teaspoonfuls onto wax paper. Cool completely. Store in an airtight container. **Yield:** 3 dozen.

Peppermint-Chocolate Truffles

Minty chocolate morsels and fluffy marshmallow cream make these foolproof truffles unforgettably luscious.

1½ cups sugar
¾ cup butter
1 (5-ounce) can evaporated milk
1⅔ cups (10 ounces) mint chocolate morsels
1 (7-ounce) jar marshmallow cream
1 teaspoon vanilla extract
6 (2-ounce) squares vanilla-flavored candy coating
⅓ cup (2 ounces) semisweet chocolate morsels
2 (2-ounce) squares vanilla-flavored candy coating, melted
Green paste food coloring

Combine first 3 ingredients in a large saucepan; bring to a boil, stirring constantly. Reduce heat, and simmer, stirring constantly, until mixture reaches soft ball stage or candy thermometer registers 234°. Remove from heat; add mint chocolate morsels, stirring until morsels melt. Stir in marshmallow cream and vanilla.

Spoon into a lightly greased 15- x 10- x 1-inch jellyroll pan; cover and chill 1 hour. Cut into 96 squares, and roll each square into a ball; chill.

Combine 6 (2-ounce) squares candy coating and semisweet chocolate morsels in a heavy saucepan. Cook over low heat until coating and morsels melt, stirring occasionally. Cool slightly.

Dip half of balls in coating mixture (keep remaining half of balls in refrigerator); place on wax paper, and cool. Repeat procedure with remaining balls and coating mixture.

Combine 2 (2-ounce) squares melted candy coating and food coloring; drizzle over truffles. Store in refrigerator. **Yield:** 8 dozen.

NOTE: Don't substitute liquid food coloring for paste food coloring in this recipe because it makes the coating too liquid. Find paste food coloring in craft stores or kitchen shops.

Chocolate Fondue
(page 108)

Sweetest of All

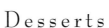

Desserts

Our glittering gallery of desserts ranges from simply sweet Chocolate Fondue to sublimely special Dark Chocolate Decadence. Frosty delights, airy soufflés, and satiny smooth custards will help you conclude your holiday meals on a satisfying sweet note.

Chocolate
Mousse Tarts

Chocolate Mousse Tarts

Whole vanilla wafers snap into place as the crusts for these cherry-topped tempters.

24 vanilla wafers
1 (8-ounce) package cream cheese, softened
1 (3-ounce) package cream cheese, softened
2/3 cup sugar
6 large eggs
8 (1-ounce) squares semisweet chocolate, melted
1/3 cup whipping cream
1 tablespoon vanilla extract
Sweetened whipped cream
Chocolate syrup
Garnish: maraschino cherries with stems

Line 24 muffin pans with paper liners. Place a vanilla wafer in each liner; set aside.

Beat cream cheese in a large mixing bowl at medium speed of an electric mixer until creamy. Gradually add sugar, beating well. Add eggs, one at a time, beating after each addition. Add melted chocolate, whipping cream, and vanilla; beat at low speed just until blended. Spoon evenly into liners.

Bake at 325° for 14 to 16 minutes. Cool in pans on wire racks. Cover and chill.

To serve, pipe or dollop sweetened whipped cream in center of tarts; drizzle with chocolate syrup. Garnish, if desired. **Yield:** 2 dozen.

Chocolate Tiramisù

1 cup sugar
1/4 cup whipping cream
4 egg yolks
1 (8-ounce) package cream cheese, softened
2 1/2 tablespoons sour cream
1/3 cup cocoa
2 tablespoons Kahlúa or other coffee-flavored liqueur or strongly brewed coffee
2/3 cup whipping cream
2 (3-ounce) packages ladyfingers
1 1/4 cups whipping cream
3 tablespoons powdered sugar
Garnish: semisweet chocolate shavings

Combine first 3 ingredients in top of a double boiler; beat at medium speed of an electric mixer until thick and pale. Bring water to a boil; reduce heat to low, and cook, stirring constantly, 8 to 10 minutes or until mixture reaches 160°. Remove from heat; cool to room temperature.

Combine cream cheese and sour cream in a large mixing bowl; beat at medium speed until smooth. Add custard mixture, cocoa, and Kahlúa, beating until smooth.

Beat 2/3 cup whipping cream until soft peaks form; fold into cream cheese mixture.

Line bottom and sides of a 9- x 5- x 3-inch loafpan with wax paper. Split ladyfingers in half lengthwise; line bottom and sides of pan with ladyfingers. Pour half of cream cheese mixture over ladyfingers in pan; top with a layer of ladyfingers. Pour remaining cream cheese mixture into pan. Arrange remaining ladyfingers on top of cream cheese mixture. Cover and chill 8 hours.

To serve, unmold onto a serving tray. Beat 1 1/4 cups whipping cream until foamy; gradually add powdered sugar, beating until soft peaks form. Pipe or dollop on top and around bottom of tiramisù. Garnish, if desired. **Yield:** 8 servings.

NOTE: Make chocolate shavings by pulling a vegetable peeler across the surface of a square of semisweet chocolate.

Chocolate-Mint
Soufflés

Chocolate-Mint Soufflés

Razzle-dazzle your guests with this marvelous chocolate mousse-like creation. A lavish dollop of Velvety Cream Sauce and crisp chocolate pastry stars will doubly delight the diners.

1 envelope unflavored gelatin
¼ cup cold water
½ cup sugar
½ cup milk
3 large eggs, lightly beaten
1 cup (6 ounces) semisweet chocolate morsels
½ teaspoon peppermint extract
1½ cups whipping cream, whipped
Velvety Cream Sauce
Chocolate Pastries

Sprinkle gelatin over water in top of a double boiler; let stand 1 minute. Add sugar, milk, and eggs; bring water in bottom of double boiler to a boil. Reduce heat to low; cook, stirring constantly, 20 minutes or until mixture slightly thickens.

Remove from heat; add morsels and extract, stirring until smooth. Cool, stirring occasionally.

Fold in whipped cream; spoon into individual serving dishes. Cover and chill. Just before serving, dollop each serving with Velvety Cream Sauce, and insert 2 pastries. **Yield:** 6 servings.

Velvety Cream Sauce
½ cup whipping cream
2½ tablespoons sifted powdered sugar
2 tablespoons sour cream
¼ teaspoon vanilla extract

Combine all ingredients; beat at high speed of a mixer until soft peaks form. **Yield:** 1¼ cups.

Chocolate Pastries
½ (15-ounce) package refrigerated piecrusts
1 (2-ounce) square chocolate-flavored candy coating, melted

Roll pastry on a lightly floured surface to remove creases. Cut into desired shapes, using 1- or 2-inch cookie cutters. Place cutouts on a lightly greased baking sheet. Bake at 400° for 6 minutes or until lightly browned. Remove from baking sheet; cool on wire racks. Drizzle with melted coating. Store in an airtight container. **Yield:** 12 pastries.

Grand Marnier Soufflé

2 tablespoons sugar
8 large eggs, separated
⅔ cup sugar
⅓ cup Grand Marnier or other orange-flavored liqueur
⅓ cup frozen orange juice concentrate, thawed and undiluted
1 teaspoon grated orange rind
Sifted powdered sugar

Cut a piece of aluminum foil long enough to fit around a 2½-quart soufflé dish, allowing a 1-inch overlap; fold foil lengthwise into thirds. Lightly butter one side of foil and bottom of dish. Wrap foil around outside of dish, buttered side against dish, allowing it to extend 3 inches above rim to form a collar. Secure with freezer tape.

Sprinkle 2 tablespoons sugar in prepared dish, tilting to coat bottom and sides; discard excess sugar. Set aside.

Beat egg yolks in top of a double boiler at medium speed of an electric mixer; gradually add ⅔ cup sugar, beating until thick and pale.

Bring water to a boil; reduce heat to low, and beat egg mixture at high speed 10 minutes or until thickened.

Stir in Grand Marnier, orange juice concentrate, and orange rind.

Cover and chill up to 8 hours.

Beat egg whites until stiff peaks form; gently fold into egg yolk mixture. Pour mixture into prepared dish.

Bake at 375° for 20 to 25 minutes or until puffed and lightly browned (center will be slightly soft). Remove from oven; sprinkle with powdered sugar. Serve immediately. **Yield:** 6 servings.

Kahlúa Soufflés

1 tablespoon sugar
Kahlúa Sauce
¼ cup butter or margarine
¼ cup all-purpose flour
1 cup milk
4 large eggs, separated
2 tablespoons Kahlúa or other coffee-
    flavored liqueur
¾ cup sugar
2 tablespoons cornstarch
Sifted powdered sugar

Butter 10 (6-ounce) custard cups; sprinkle with 1 tablespoon sugar, tilting to coat bottom and sides. Spoon Kahlúa Sauce into each cup.

Melt ¼ cup butter in a large saucepan over low heat; add flour, stirring until smooth. Cook 1 minute, stirring constantly. Gradually add milk; cook, stirring constantly, until mixture thickens and begins to leave sides of pan. Remove from heat; cool 15 minutes. Add yolks, one at a time, beating after each addition. Stir in Kahlúa; set aside.

Combine ¾ cup sugar and cornstarch; set aside. Beat egg whites at high speed of an electric mixer until foamy. Gradually add sugar mixture, 1 tablespoon at a time, beating until stiff peaks form and sugar dissolves (2 to 4 minutes). Gradually stir one-fourth of yolk mixture into whites; gently fold into remaining yolk mixture. Spoon evenly over Kahlúa Sauce in cups; place cups in a large shallow pan. Pour hot water into pan to depth of 1 inch. Bake, uncovered, at 400° for 10 minutes. Reduce oven temperature to 350°, and bake 20 additional minutes or until golden.

Remove cups from water; sprinkle with powdered sugar. Serve immediately. **Yield:** 10 servings.

NOTE: To make ahead, use freezer-to-oven dishes. Wrap dishes in heavy-duty aluminum foil before baking; freeze up to 2 weeks. Place frozen soufflés in shallow pan. Pour hot water into pan to depth of 1 inch. Bake, uncovered, at 400° for 10 minutes. Reduce temperature to 350°; bake 40 minutes or until golden.

Kahlúa Sauce

⅓ cup sugar
⅓ cup water
3 tablespoons light corn syrup
¼ cup cocoa
2 tablespoons Kahlúa or other coffee-
    flavored liqueur

Combine first 3 ingredients; bring to a boil. Boil 1 minute, stirring constantly. Remove from heat; stir in cocoa and Kahlúa. **Yield:** ¾ cup.

Dark Chocolate Decadence

1 (9-ounce) package chocolate wafers, crushed
1 (3½-ounce) can flaked coconut (1½ cups)
⅓ cup butter or margarine, melted
¼ cup butter or margarine, softened
¾ cup firmly packed brown sugar
3 large eggs
2 teaspoons instant coffee granules
2 tablespoons hot water
2 cups (12 ounces) semisweet chocolate
    morsels, melted
1 cup cashews, coarsely chopped
¼ cup all-purpose flour
1 cup whipping cream, whipped
Garnish: chopped cashews

Combine chocolate wafer crumbs and coconut; stir in ⅓ cup butter. Firmly press mixture in bottom and 1 inch up sides of a greased 9-inch springform pan.

Beat ¼ cup butter at medium speed of an electric mixer until creamy; gradually add sugar, beating until blended. Add eggs, one at a time, beating just until yellow disappears.

Dissolve coffee in hot water; add to butter mixture. Stir in melted chocolate morsels, 1 cup cashews, and flour. Spoon into prepared crust.

Bake at 375° for 25 minutes. (Wooden pick inserted in center will not come out clean.) Cool in pan on a wire rack. Cover and chill 8 hours.

Dollop whipped cream around top edge of dessert. Garnish, if desired. **Yield:** 10 servings.

White Chocolate Brownie
with Hot Fudge Sauce

White Chocolate Brownies with Hot Fudge Sauce

If you don't have time to make the Hot Fudge Sauce, serve these almond- and white chocolate-studded brownies solo. They'll satisfy any sweet tooth on their own.

2 (6-ounce) packages white baking bar,
 coarsely chopped*
2 large eggs
½ cup sugar
¼ cup butter or margarine, melted
1 teaspoon vanilla extract
1 cup all-purpose flour
¼ teaspoon salt
1 (6-ounce) package white baking bar,
 coarsely chopped*
½ cup chopped almonds, toasted, or
 chopped macadamia nuts
Hot Fudge Sauce

Place 12 ounces baking bar in a heavy saucepan; cook over low heat, stirring constantly, until baking bar melts. Remove from heat; let stand 10 minutes.

Beat eggs in a small mixing bowl at high speed of an electric mixer until foamy. Gradually add sugar, 1 tablespoon at a time, beating 2 to 4 minutes. Stir in melted baking bar, butter, and vanilla. (Mixture may appear curdled.) Add flour and salt, stirring until blended. Stir in 6 ounces chopped baking bar and almonds.

Spoon batter into a greased and floured 13- x 9- x 2-inch pan. Bake at 350° for 25 minutes. Cool and cut into squares. Serve with warm Hot Fudge Sauce. **Yield:** 12 servings.

Hot Fudge Sauce
⅔ cup whipping cream
¼ cup sugar
1 (4-ounce) bar bittersweet chocolate,
 chopped, or 4 (1-ounce) squares
 semisweet chocolate, chopped
1½ tablespoons butter or margarine
1½ tablespoons light corn syrup

Combine whipping cream and sugar in a small heavy saucepan; cook over low heat, stirring constantly, until sugar dissolves. Add chocolate, stirring until chocolate melts. Add butter and corn syrup, stirring until butter melts. **Yield:** 1⅓ cups.

* For white baking bars, we used Nestlé Premier White Baking Bars.

Bourbon-Pecan Macaroon Bombe

Quick Caramel Sauce is the perfect companion for this frozen dessert, but don't stop there. It also makes an incredible ice cream or pound cake topper.

4½ cups soft coconut macaroon cookie
      crumbs (about 23 cookies)*
¼ cup bourbon
Vegetable cooking spray
1 (8-ounce) package cream cheese, softened
1 (14-ounce) can sweetened condensed milk
1 (12-ounce) container frozen whipped
      topping, thawed
1 cup pecan pieces, toasted
Quick Caramel Sauce

Place cookie crumbs in a bowl. Drizzle with bourbon; toss. Let stand 30 minutes.

Coat a 9-cup mold with cooking spray; line with plastic wrap. Press bourbon-soaked crumbs into mold, forming a shell; set aside.

Combine cream cheese and sweetened condensed milk in a large mixing bowl; beat at medium speed of an electric mixer until smooth. Fold in whipped topping and pecans. Spoon into prepared shell. Cover and freeze until firm.

To serve, invert bombe onto a chilled serving platter. Place a damp, warm towel around mold. Remove mold; peel off plastic wrap. Slice into wedges. Serve with Quick Caramel Sauce. **Yield:** 10 servings.

Quick Caramel Sauce
1 (12-ounce) jar caramel topping
1 tablespoon butter or margarine
2 tablespoons bourbon (optional)

Combine caramel topping and butter in a small saucepan; cook over medium heat, stirring constantly, until butter melts and sauce is thoroughly heated. Remove from heat, and stir in bourbon, if desired. Cool slightly. **Yield:** 1 cup.

* For soft coconut macaroon cookies, we used 2 (13.75-ounce) packages of Archway cookies.

Caramel-Ice Cream Tart

¾ cup firmly packed brown sugar
1 large egg, beaten
2 tablespoons butter or margarine, melted
1 teaspoon vanilla extract
⅛ teaspoon salt
⅓ cup all-purpose flour
¼ teaspoon baking soda
1 cup chopped pecans
½ gallon vanilla ice cream, softened
Nutty Caramel Sauce

Line a 9-inch springform pan with aluminum foil, folding edges over rim. Generously coat foil with butter.

Combine first 5 ingredients in a bowl; add flour and soda, stirring until blended. Stir in pecans. Spread in prepared pan. Bake at 350° for 25 minutes or until edges are barely firm. Cool in pan on a wire rack. Gently loosen foil from pan, and lift shell from pan; carefully remove foil. Wrap shell in foil until ready to serve.

Line same 9-inch springform pan with foil or plastic wrap. Spread ice cream in pan; cover and freeze. Lift ice cream from pan; remove foil.

To serve, place shell on a serving platter; top with ice cream layer. Cut into serving-size pieces, and drizzle with Nutty Caramel Sauce. **Yield:** one 9-inch tart.

Nutty Caramel Sauce
1 cup sugar
½ cup butter or margarine
½ cup half-and-half
½ cup chopped pecans, toasted

Place sugar in a cast-iron skillet. Cook over medium heat, stirring constantly with a wooden spoon, until sugar turns golden. Remove from heat; add butter, stirring until butter melts.

Return mixture to low heat; gradually add half-and-half, 1 tablespoon at a time, stirring constantly. Cook, stirring constantly, 3 minutes or until thickened and creamy. Stir in pecans. Cool slightly. **Yield:** 1½ cups.

Chocolate-Coffee Ice Cream Torte

Chewy coconut cookies, coffee ice cream, and toffee-flavored candy bars collide deliciously in this decadent dessert.

6 soft coconut macaroon cookies, crumbled*
2 tablespoons butter or margarine, melted
1 quart chocolate ice cream, softened
½ cup chocolate syrup, divided
4 (1.4-ounce) English toffee-flavored candy
       bars, crushed and divided*
1 quart coffee or vanilla ice cream, softened

Combine cookie crumbs and butter in a bowl; firmly press mixture in bottom of a 9-inch spring-form pan.

Spread chocolate ice cream over crust; drizzle with half of chocolate syrup, and sprinkle with half of crushed candy. Freeze until firm.

Spread coffee ice cream over crushed candy in crust; drizzle with remaining chocolate syrup, and sprinkle with remaining crushed candy. Cover and freeze.

To serve, carefully remove sides of springform pan. Cut into wedges. **Yield:** 12 servings.

* For soft coconut macaroon cookies, we used Archway, and for English toffee-flavored candy bars, we used Heath bars.

Cranberry Sherbet

1 (12-ounce) package fresh cranberries
       (3 cups)
1 cup sugar
¾ cup water
½ cup orange juice
¾ cup half-and-half
4 ice cubes
2 tablespoons lemon juice

Combine first 4 ingredients in a saucepan; bring to a boil. Reduce heat, and simmer 6 to 8 minutes or until cranberry skins pop. Let cool.

Pour mixture into container of an electric blender; process until smooth, stopping once to scrape down sides. Pour mixture through a wire-mesh strainer into a bowl, discarding skins. Return cranberry puree to blender. Add half-and-half and remaining ingredients; process until smooth, stopping once to scrape down sides.

Pour mixture into an 8-inch square pan; cover and freeze 2 hours or until slushy. Spoon into a large mixing bowl; beat at medium speed of an electric mixer until fluffy. Repeat freezing and beating procedure once. Return mixture to pan; cover and freeze until firm.

To serve, scoop into individual dessert dishes. Serve immediately. **Yield:** 4 cups.

Raspberry-Beaujolais Sorbet

3 cups frozen raspberries, thawed
½ cup water
¾ cup sugar
1 cup Beaujolais or other dry red wine
¼ cup whipping cream
2 tablespoons lemon juice

Combine raspberries and water in container of an electric blender; process until smooth, stopping once to scrape down sides. Pour mixture through a wire-mesh strainer into a bowl, pressing raspberries with back of a spoon against the sides of the strainer to squeeze out juice; discard raspberry pulp and seeds.

Return raspberry juice to blender; add sugar and remaining ingredients. Process 1 minute, stopping once to scrape down sides.

Pour mixture into a 9-inch square pan; cover and freeze until almost firm. Break into chunks, and place in a large mixing bowl; beat at low speed of an electric mixer until smooth. Return mixture to pan; cover and freeze until firm.

To serve, scoop into individual dessert dishes. Serve immediately. **Yield:** 3 cups.

Honey Bear Bread
(page 133)

Gingerbread Cookies
(page 128)

Elfin Delights

———— ❧ ————

Children's Favorites

Create magical memories for Santa's little helpers with these tailor-made recipes. You'll enjoy baking cuddly teddy bear bread, artful angel cookies, or ice cream cone cupcakes as much as the children. You're bound to receive appreciative hugs in return.

Simple
Fruit Punch

Cracker
Snack Mix

Fruit and Cheese
Kabobs

Santa's
Boot Cookie
(page 128)

Party Peanut
Butter Sandwiches
(page 129)

Simple Fruit Punch

A few drops of red food coloring transform this lemon and pineapple punch into red and rambunctious party fare.

1 (5-ounce) package lemonade-flavored drink
    mix
1 (46-ounce) can unsweetened pineapple
    juice, chilled
1 (1-liter) bottle ginger ale, chilled
Red liquid food coloring (optional)

Prepare drink mix according to package directions; chill.

Stir in pineapple juice and ginger ale just before serving; add a few drops of food coloring, if desired. **Yield:** 4½ quarts.

Fruit and Cheese Kabobs

1 (8-ounce) can unsweetened pineapple
    chunks
1 large apple, unpeeled and cut into ¾-inch
    pieces
12 whole fresh strawberries
12 seedless grapes
12 (¾-inch) cubes Cheddar cheese
12 (6-inch) thin plastic drinking straws

Drain pineapple, reserving juice. Combine juice and apple, tossing to coat. Thread fruit and cheese onto straws. **Yield:** 12 servings.

Cracker Snack Mix

2 cups small pretzels
2 cups goldfish-shaped crackers
1 cup bite-size Cheddar cheese crackers
1 cup crisp rice cereal squares*
3 tablespoons butter or margarine, melted
2 teaspoons Worcestershire sauce
½ teaspoon seasoned salt

Combine first 4 ingredients in a large bowl. Combine melted butter, Worcestershire sauce, and seasoned salt; pour over pretzel mixture, tossing to coat.

Spread in a 15- x 10- x 1-inch jellyroll pan. Bake at 250° for 30 minutes, stirring twice. Cool. Store in an airtight container. **Yield:** 6 cups.

* For crisp rice cereal squares, we used Rice Chex.

Little Buckaroo Snacks

Round up your little cowboys and cowgirls for this funtime snack. They'll enjoy capturing the animal-shaped crackers lurking behind boulders of peanuts, candy-coated chocolate pieces, and raisins.

2 cups animal-shaped graham crackers
1 cup dry roasted peanuts
½ cup candy-coated chocolate pieces or
    jelly beans
½ cup raisins

Combine all ingredients; store in an airtight container. **Yield:** 3½ cups.

People Chow

1 (11½-ounce) package milk chocolate
    morsels
1 cup creamy peanut butter
½ cup butter or margarine
1 (13-ounce) box honey graham cereal
3 cups sifted powdered sugar

Combine first 3 ingredients in a large
saucepan; cook over low heat, stirring constantly,
until mixture is smooth.
   Remove from heat; add cereal, stirring gently
to coat.
   Place half the powdered sugar in a large heavy-
duty, zip-top plastic bag; add cereal mixture and
remaining half of powdered sugar. Seal bag, and
shake gently to coat.
   Pour mixture onto two ungreased cookie
sheets; let stand at room temperature until dry.
Separate large pieces with a fork, if necessary.
Yield: 12 cups.

Fudge Drops

1 (11½-ounce) package milk chocolate
    morsels
1¼ cups granola cereal
1 cup salted peanuts
Garnishes: candied cherries, candy-coated
    chocolate pieces

Place milk chocolate morsels in a microwave-
safe bowl; microwave at MEDIUM (50% power)
2 minutes. Stir in granola cereal and peanuts.
Drop by teaspoonfuls onto wax paper-lined cookie
sheets. Garnish, if desired. Chill until firm. **Yield:**
4 dozen.

Easy Reindeer Cookies

*Rudolph would glow with pride over these easy-to-
shape cookies bearing his likeness.*

1 (20-ounce) package refrigerated sliceable
    peanut butter cookie dough
60 (2-inch) pretzel twists
60 semisweet chocolate morsels
30 red candy-coated chocolate pieces

Freeze dough 15 minutes. Cut dough into
30 (¼-inch-thick) slices. Place 4 inches apart on
ungreased cookie sheets. Using thumb and fore-
finger, pinch in each slice about two-thirds of the
way down to shape face.
   Press a pretzel on each side of larger end for
antlers. Press in chocolate morsels for eyes.
   Bake at 350° for 9 to 11 minutes or until
lightly browned.
   Remove from oven, and press in red candy for
nose. Cool on cookie sheets 2 minutes; transfer to
wire racks to cool. **Yield:** 2½ dozen.

People Chow

Easy Reindeer
Cookies

Christmas
Mice Cookies

Christmas Mice Cookies

These winsome creatures will cause a stir all through the house. Their little ears are made of peanut halves, eyes of cinnamon candies, and tails of red licorice.

½   cup butter or margarine, softened
1   cup creamy peanut butter
½   cup firmly packed brown sugar
½   cup sugar
1   large egg
1   teaspoon vanilla extract
1½ cups all-purpose flour
½   teaspoon baking soda
Dry roasted peanuts
1   (2.25-ounce) jar red cinnamon candies
4   yards thin red licorice, cut into 3-inch
      pieces

Beat butter and peanut butter in a large mixing bowl at medium speed of an electric mixer until creamy; gradually add sugars, beating well. Add egg and vanilla, beating well.

Combine flour and soda; gradually add to butter mixture, beating until blended. Cover and chill at least 2 hours.

Shape dough into 1-inch balls; taper 1 end of each ball to form a teardrop shape. Press 1 side flat; place cookies, flat sides down, 2 inches apart on ungreased cookie sheets. Gently press in sides of dough to raise backs of mice. Gently place 2 peanut halves in dough for ears. With a wooden pick, make a ½-inch-deep hole at tail end.

Bake at 350° for 9 minutes. Remove from oven, and carefully place red cinnamon candies in cookies for eyes. Return to oven, and bake 1 to 2 additional minutes or until browned. Remove from oven; insert licorice tails. Cool on cookie sheets on wire racks. **Yield:** 4 dozen.

Teddy Bear Cookies

You'd be hard pressed to find something more appealing than these dapper teddy bears. They easily don their red bow ties and white buttons with decorator frosting.

⅓   cup butter or margarine, softened
1   cup sugar
2   large eggs
2   (1-ounce) squares unsweetened chocolate,
      melted
2   teaspoons vanilla extract
2½ cups all-purpose flour
½   teaspoon baking soda
½   teaspoon salt
1   (4.25-ounce) tube red decorator frosting
1   (4.25-ounce) tube white decorator frosting

Beat butter in a large mixing bowl at medium speed of an electric mixer until creamy; gradually add sugar, beating well. Add eggs, one at a time, beating after each addition. Stir in melted chocolate and vanilla.

Combine flour, soda, and salt; gradually add to butter mixture, beating until blended. Cover and chill 2 hours.

Divide dough into 12 balls. For bear's body, cut a ball of dough in half; shape one-half into a ball. Place on an ungreased cookie sheet, and flatten into a 3- x 2½-inch oval.

Cut remaining half into 2 equal portions. For bear's head, shape 1 portion into a round ball, and flatten on cookie sheet, slightly overlapping body. Pinch off a small piece from remaining portion for nose; position on head.

Roll remaining dough into a 5-inch-long rope. Cut 2 (½-inch) pieces for ears and 4 (1-inch) pieces for legs. Roll each piece into a ball. Attach ears and legs to bear's body; flatten slightly. Repeat procedure with remaining dough balls.

Bake at 350° for 10 minutes or until almost set. Cool on cookie sheets on wire racks. Remove from cookie sheets, and decorate with frosting. **Yield:** 1 dozen.

Christmas Cupcakes

Turn your little artists loose on these cupcakes, and they'll turn each one into a masterpiece. Provide a full palette of decorator candies to spark their creativity. Gummy Bears, licorice, and red cinnamon candies are just a few of the possibilities.

1 (16-ounce) package pound cake mix
¾ cup milk
2 large eggs
½ teaspoon vanilla extract
1 (16-ounce) container ready-to-spread   ·
     vanilla frosting
Assorted candies

Combine first 4 ingredients in a large mixing bowl; beat at medium speed of an electric mixer 4 minutes.

Spoon evenly into paper-lined muffin pans. Bake at 350° for 16 to 18 minutes or until a wooden pick inserted in center comes out clean. Remove from pans immediately, and cool on wire racks.

Spread tops of cupcakes with frosting, and decorate with candies. **Yield:** 16 cupcakes.

NOTE: To make chocolate cupcakes, add ¾ cup chocolate syrup to batter. Yield: 21 cupcakes.

Santa Claus Cupcakes

A fluffy white coconut beard, jolly red cinnamon nose, and twinkling candy eyes make Santa Claus come to life—cupcake fashion.

1 (18.25-ounce) package white cake mix
     with pudding
18 flat-bottomed jumbo "cake cup" ice
     cream cones
1 (16-ounce) container ready-to-spread
     cream cheese frosting
Flaked coconut
Miniature marshmallows
Red cinnamon candies
Miniature candy-coated chocolate pieces

Prepare cake mix according to package directions. Spoon 5 tablespoons batter into each cone; place cones in muffin pans.

Bake at 350° for 25 to 27 minutes or until a wooden pick inserted in center of cupcakes comes out clean. Remove cones from pans, and cool on wire racks.

Spread tops of cupcakes with cream cheese frosting, and decorate with flaked coconut and remaining ingredients. (Do not store cupcakes in an airtight container or the cones will become soft.) **Yield:** 1½ dozen.

Santa Claus
Cupcakes

Candied Cereal Pizza

1 (10½-ounce) package miniature
    marshmallows
8 ounces vanilla-flavored candy coating,
    finely chopped
¼ cup butter or margarine
¼ cup light corn syrup
6 cups crisp rice cereal*
1 cup dry roasted peanuts
Hard peppermint candies
Red cinnamon candies
Thin red licorice

Combine first 4 ingredients in a heavy sauce-pan; cook over low heat, stirring constantly, until smooth. Stir in cereal and peanuts. Cool to touch.

Spoon onto an ungreased 12-inch pizza pan; shape into a circle, slightly mounding sides. Decorate with candies and licorice, pressing into cereal mixture. Cool completely. Remove from pan. **Yield:** one 12-inch cereal pizza.

NOTE: Turn the Candied Cereal Pizza into a gift with pizzazz by placing it in a real pizza box that you decorate in yuletide style. Unfold a 12-inch pizza box, and lay it completely flat. Coat outside with spray paint; let dry. Cut designs from holiday wrapping paper, and attach to box with spray adhesive or glue. Refold box.

* For crisp rice cereal, we used Kellogg's Rice Krispies.

Candied Cereal
Pizza

Honey Bear Bread (photo on page 120)

Tie a jaunty ribbon around the neck of each of these sweet honey bears for a merry holiday touch.

2 packages active dry yeast
½ cup warm water (105° to 115°)
1½ cups warm water (105° to 115°)
¼ cup vegetable oil
¼ cup honey
2 large eggs, beaten
1 tablespoon sugar
2 teaspoons salt
2 cups whole wheat flour
1 cup regular oats, uncooked
3¼ to 3¾ cups all-purpose flour
6 raisins
1½ tablespoons butter or margarine, melted

Combine yeast and ½ cup warm water in a 1-cup liquid measuring cup; let stand 5 minutes.

Remove yeast mixture to a large mixing bowl. Add 1½ cups warm water and next 5 ingredients; stir well.

Add wheat flour, and beat at medium speed of an electric mixer until blended. Gradually stir in oats and enough all-purpose flour to make a soft dough.

Turn dough out onto a floured surface, and knead until smooth and elastic (about 8 to 10 minutes). Place in a well-greased bowl, turning to grease top.

Cover and let rise in a warm place (85°), free from drafts, 1 hour or until doubled in bulk.

Punch dough down, and divide in half. Set 1 portion aside. Divide dough in half. Shape half into a smooth ball for bear's body, and place on a lightly greased baking sheet. Divide remaining half into 4 equal portions. Shape 1 portion into a round ball, and position on baking sheet for bear's head. Shape another portion into two 1-inch balls for ears, and attach to head, flattening slightly. Divide and shape remaining 2 portions into arms and legs, and attach to bear's body. Repeat procedure with reserved portion of dough.

Position raisins for eyes and noses. Cover and let rise in a warm place, free from drafts, 20 to 30 minutes or until doubled in bulk.

Bake at 350° for 20 to 25 minutes or until loaves sound hollow when tapped. Remove from oven; brush with melted butter. Transfer to wire racks to cool. **Yield:** 2 loaves.

Christmas Popcorn

1 cup butter or margarine
¾ cup sugar
1 (3-ounce) package cherry-flavored gelatin
3 tablespoons water
1 tablespoon light corn syrup
10 cups popped popcorn

Combine butter, sugar, gelatin, water, and corn syrup in a heavy 2-quart saucepan; bring to a boil over medium heat, stirring constantly. Cook until mixture reaches hard ball stage or candy thermometer registers 255°, stirring occasionally.

Place popped popcorn in a large bowl; pour hot gelatin mixture over popcorn, and stir gently until coated.

Spoon into a large baking pan. Bake at 300° for 10 minutes, stirring twice.

Remove to a sheet of lightly greased aluminum foil, and let cool. Break into clusters. **Yield:** 5 cups.

Honeyed
Peach Glaze
(page 145)

Cherry
Treats
(page 140)

Herb and
Pepper Cheese
Spread
(page 152)

Making a List

Gifts from the Kitchen

A gift from the heart of your home is always appreciated and unique. Try a glistening jar of honeyed glaze, beribboned box of cherry muffins, or shapely container of herbed cheese spread. Creative packaging ideas will make these super gifts for the special people in your life even more appealing.

Orange Almonds

1½ cups whole blanched almonds, lightly
    toasted
1 egg white, lightly beaten
¾ cup sifted powdered sugar
1½ teaspoons grated orange rind
Dash of ground nutmeg

Combine almonds and egg white in a bowl;
set aside.

Combine powdered sugar, orange rind, and
nutmeg. Drain almonds; add to powdered sugar
mixture, stirring until coated.

Place in a single layer on a greased baking
sheet. Bake at 250° for 20 to 30 minutes or until
coating is dry and almonds are crisp, stirring occasionally. **Yield:** 1½ cups.

Pepper Nuts

*A fiery blend of three ground peppers—white,
red, and black—enkindles these buttery toasted
almonds.*

2 (6-ounce) cans whole natural almonds
3 tablespoons butter or margarine
3 tablespoons white wine Worcestershire
    sauce*
1 teaspoon salt
1 teaspoon chili powder
½ teaspoon garlic powder
⅛ teaspoon ground white pepper
⅛ teaspoon ground red pepper
⅛ teaspoon black pepper

Place whole almonds in a medium bowl, and
set aside.

Melt butter in a small saucepan over medium
heat. Add Worcestershire sauce and remaining
6 ingredients, stirring well to combine. Cook
1 minute, stirring occasionally.

Pour butter mixture over almonds, stirring
gently to coat. Let almond mixture stand at room
temperature 30 minutes.

Place almond mixture in a single layer in an
ungreased 15- x 10- x 1-inch jellyroll pan. Bake
at 300° for 35 minutes, stirring often. Cool.
Yield: 2 cups.

* You can substitute regular Worcestershire sauce
if you don't have the white wine variety, but the
nuts will be very dark in color. The lighter white
wine Worcestershire sauce yields a prettier color.

Mexican Snack Mix

*Semisweet chocolate morsels and raisins play off the
spiciness of chili powder and red pepper in this
munchable mix.*

1 (12.2-ounce) package mini shredded whole
    wheat cereal biscuits*
1 (12-ounce) can mixed nuts
1 (6.5-ounce) package pretzel twists*
⅓ cup butter or margarine, melted
1 tablespoon chili powder
¾ teaspoon garlic powder
½ teaspoon ground red pepper
1 cup raisins
¾ cup (4½ ounces) semisweet chocolate
    morsels

Combine first 3 ingredients in a large bowl;
drizzle with butter, stirring gently to coat.

Combine chili powder, garlic powder, and red
pepper; sprinkle over cereal mixture, stirring gently to coat.

Place in an ungreased 15- x 10- x 1-inch
jellyroll pan. Bake at 250° for 20 minutes, stirring every 5 minutes. Cool. Stir in raisins and
chocolate morsels. Store in an airtight container.
Yield: 15 cups.

* For mini shredded whole wheat cereal biscuits,
we used Nabisco Spoon-Size Shredded Wheat,
and for pretzel twists, we used Planter's brand.

Sugar and
Spice Gorp

Sugar and Spice Gorp

Squirrel away empty peanut cans to create tailor-made gift containers.

1 egg white
1 tablespoon butter or margarine, melted
1 (12-ounce) can cocktail peanuts
1⅓ cups sugar
1 tablespoon plus 1 teaspoon ground
      cinnamon
2 teaspoons ground nutmeg
1 teaspoon ground allspice
Vegetable cooking spray
1 cup candy-coated chocolate pieces
½ cup raisins
½ cup coarsely chopped dried apricot halves

Beat egg white in a large mixing bowl at high speed of an electric mixer until stiff peaks form; stir in butter. Add peanuts, tossing to coat.

Combine sugar and next 3 ingredients in a large heavy-duty, zip-top plastic bag. Add ¼ cup coated peanuts to sugar mixture; seal bag, and shake gently to coat.

Use a slotted spoon to remove sugar-coated peanuts to a baking sheet coated with cooking spray. Repeat procedure with remaining sugar mixture and coated peanuts.

Bake at 300° for 20 minutes, stirring after 10 minutes. Cool.

Combine sugar-coated peanuts, chocolate pieces, and remaining ingredients. **Yield:** 5 cups.

Chocolate-Mint Truffles

A tiny bite of these exquisite minted candies reveals a velvety blend of chocolate, whipping cream, and butter enveloped in a smooth chocolate shell. A lacy drizzle of vanilla coating atop each truffle adds a dainty diversion.

1⅔ cups whipping cream
½ cup unsalted butter
1 pound semisweet chocolate, coarsely
    chopped
2 tablespoons crème de menthe
12 ounces chocolate-flavored candy coating
4 ounces vanilla-flavored candy coating,
    melted

Combine whipping cream and butter in a heavy saucepan; cook over low heat, stirring constantly, until butter melts. Bring to a boil. Remove from heat.

Add semisweet chocolate, stirring until chocolate melts and mixture is thickened and smooth. Stir in crème de menthe. Cover and chill 3 to 4 hours, stirring every 30 minutes or until mixture begins to become firm.

Divide mixture into 3 portions. (Work with 1 portion at a time, storing remaining portions in refrigerator.) Working quickly, drop chocolate mixture by heaping teaspoonfuls onto a wax paper-lined 15- x 10- x 1-inch jellyroll pan; freeze 10 minutes. Repeat procedure with remaining portions.

Place chocolate-flavored candy coating in top of a double boiler; bring water to a boil. Reduce heat to low; cook until chocolate candy coating melts, stirring occasionally. Remove double boiler from heat.

Remove 1 portion of chocolate mixture from freezer; shape into balls. Place each ball on a candy fork, and quickly spoon chocolate candy coating generously over ball, tapping fork briefly on edge of bowl to remove excess coating. (Be careful not to let any of the chocolate mixture drip into the chocolate candy coating.) Remove truffles from dipping fork with a knife, and place on wax paper. Freeze 10 minutes. Repeat procedure with remaining chocolate mixture and chocolate candy coating.

Use a fork to drizzle melted vanilla candy coating over truffles. Store in refrigerator. **Yield:** 4½ dozen.

NOTE: For a more precise drizzle of vanilla-flavored candy coating atop the truffles, place the melted coating in a small zip-top plastic bag. Snip a tiny hole in a corner of the bag, and use as a piping bag.

Yogurt-Praline Candy

Butter-flavored vegetable cooking spray
1 cup firmly packed brown sugar
½ cup sugar
½ cup nonfat plain yogurt
2 cups walnut or pecan halves
1 teaspoon vanilla extract

Coat a large sheet of wax paper with cooking spray; set aside.

Combine sugars and yogurt in a medium saucepan. Bring to a boil over medium heat. (Do not stir.) Boil 2 to 3 minutes or until mixture reaches thread stage or candy thermometer registers 232°.

Remove from heat; stir in walnuts and vanilla. Spoon evenly onto prepared wax paper; let stand until firm. Break into small pieces. Store in an airtight container. **Yield:** 1½ pounds.

Hot Raisin Scones

Create a dazzling present by placing each scone round on an 8-inch cake board; wrap with heavy-duty plastic wrap, and tie with a frilly ribbon.

2 cups all-purpose flour
2 teaspoons baking powder
½ teaspoon baking soda
¼ teaspoon salt
2 tablespoons sugar
1 teaspoon grated lemon rind
½ cup butter or margarine
½ cup raisins
¾ cup buttermilk

Combine first 6 ingredients in a large bowl; cut in butter with pastry blender until mixture is crumbly. Add raisins, tossing lightly to coat. Add buttermilk, stirring until dry ingredients are moistened.

Turn dough out onto a lightly floured surface, and knead lightly 6 times. Divide dough in half. Shape each portion into a 7-inch circle on an ungreased baking sheet; cut each circle into 6 wedges (do not separate).

Bake at 425° for 10 minutes. Transfer as a circle to wire racks to cool. **Yield:** 1 dozen.

NOTE: You can freeze the scones up to a month.

Yogurt-Praline
Candy

Pear Honey
(page 145)

Hot Raisin
Scones

Applesauce-Spice Mini Muffins

1 (7-ounce) package apple-cinnamon
    muffin mix
½ teaspoon ground allspice
½ cup milk
¼ cup applesauce
Sifted powdered sugar

Combine muffin mix and allspice in a large bowl; make a well in center of mixture. Add milk and applesauce, stirring just until dry ingredients are moistened.

Spoon into paper-lined miniature (1¾-inch) muffin pans, filling three-fourths full.

Bake at 425° for 10 to 12 minutes. Remove from pans immediately; sprinkle with powdered sugar. **Yield:** 2 dozen.

Cherry Treats (photo on page 134)

½ cup butter or margarine, softened
¾ cup sugar
¾ cup firmly packed brown sugar
2 eggs
2 cups all-purpose flour
1 teaspoon baking powder
½ cup maraschino cherry juice
½ cup chopped maraschino cherries
¼ cup chopped pecans
Sifted powdered sugar

Beat butter in a large mixing bowl at medium speed of an electric mixer until creamy; gradually add ¾ cup sugar and brown sugar, beating well. Add eggs, beating until blended.

Combine flour and baking powder; add to butter mixture alternately with cherry juice, beginning and ending with flour mixture. Stir in cherries.

Spoon into paper-lined miniature (1¾-inch) muffin pans, filling three-fourths full. Sprinkle evenly with pecans. Bake at 400° for 10 to 12 minutes or until lightly browned. Remove from pans immediately, and cool on wire racks. Sprinkle with powdered sugar. **Yield:** 4 dozen.

Snowflake Cupcakes

1 cup butter or margarine, softened
1½ cups sugar
3 large eggs
2 cups all-purpose flour
½ cup milk
1 teaspoon vanilla extract
Sifted powdered sugar

Beat butter until creamy; gradually add sugar, beating well. Add eggs, one at a time, beating after each addition. Add flour to butter mixture alternately with milk, beginning and ending with flour. Mix after each addition. Stir in vanilla.

Spoon into paper-lined miniature (1¾-inch) muffin pans, filling two-thirds full. Bake at 375° for 10 minutes or until a wooden pick inserted in center comes out clean. Remove from pans; cool on wire racks. Sprinkle with sugar. **Yield:** 5 dozen.

Pumpkin-Mincemeat Bread

3½ cups all-purpose flour
2 teaspoons baking soda
1½ teaspoons salt
1½ cups sugar
1½ cups firmly packed brown sugar
2 tablespoons pumpkin pie spice
4 large eggs
1 (16-ounce) can pumpkin (2 cups)
1 cup vegetable oil
⅔ cup water
1½ cups prepared mincemeat
1 cup chopped pecans

Combine first 6 ingredients; make a well in center. Combine eggs and next 3 ingredients; add to flour mixture, stirring just until moistened. Stir in mincemeat and pecans. Spoon into three greased 8½- x 4½- x 3-inch loafpans.

Bake at 350° for 1 hour or until a wooden pick inserted in center comes out clean. Cool in pans on wire racks 10 minutes; remove from pans, and cool on wire racks. **Yield:** 3 loaves.

Chocolate Chip
Pie Mix

Chocolate Chip Pie Mix

1 cup sugar
½ cup all-purpose flour
1 cup (6 ounces) semisweet chocolate
     morsels
½ cup flaked coconut
½ cup chopped pecans

   Combine sugar and flour; seal in an airtight plastic bag. Place chocolate morsels, coconut, and pecans in an airtight plastic bag; seal. Place both bags in a gift container. **Yield:** 1 (2-bag) gift.

DIRECTIONS FOR GIFT CARD: Combine ¼ cup melted butter, dry ingredient packet, and 2 large eggs; stir until dry ingredients are moistened. Stir in chocolate packet. Spoon into an unbaked 9-inch pastry shell. Bake at 350° for 35 to 40 minutes. Yield: one 9-inch pie.

Hot Cocoa
Mix

Minted Coffee Mix

¼ cup instant coffee granules
¼ cup powdered nondairy coffee creamer
⅓ cup sugar
2 tablespoons cocoa
1½ tablespoons crushed hard peppermint
    candy

Combine all ingredients in container of an electric blender; process until blended. Store in an airtight container. **Yield:** 1 cup.

DIRECTIONS FOR GIFT CARD: Combine 2 tablespoons Minted Coffee Mix with ¾ cup boiling water, stirring well. Yield: ¾ cup.

Spiced Tea Punch Mix

1 (21.1-ounce) container instant orange-
    flavored breakfast beverage crystals*
1½ cups sugar
¾ cup instant tea with lemon
1½ teaspoons ground cloves
1½ teaspoons ground cinnamon

Combine all ingredients; store in an airtight container. **Yield:** 5 cups.

DIRECTIONS FOR GIFT CARD: Combine ¾ cup Spiced Tea Punch Mix, 8 cups unsweetened pineapple juice, 8 cups apple juice, and 4 cups water in a Dutch oven. Bring to a boil; reduce heat, and simmer 15 minutes, stirring occasionally. Serve warm. Yield: 1¼ gallons.

* For instant orange-flavored breakfast beverage crystals, we used Tang.

Hot Cocoa Mix

Give a friend the joy of hot cocoa—enough for a warming mugful every day of the week. Our minted interpretation tastes like a Peppermint Patty. Place this custom-made cocoa mix in a plastic bag, and tuck it inside a holiday mug.

1 cup powdered nondairy coffee creamer
1 cup sifted powdered sugar
½ cup miniature marshmallows
¼ cup cocoa
¼ cup mint chocolate morsels

Combine all ingredients; store in an airtight container. **Yield:** 2⅓ cups.

DIRECTIONS FOR GIFT CARD: Combine ⅓ cup Hot Cocoa Mix with ⅔ cup boiling water, stirring well. Yield: about 1 cup.

New Year's Day Chili Mix

1 (16-ounce) package dried kidney beans
1 tablespoon instant minced onion
2 teaspoons beef-flavored bouillon granules
1 teaspoon salt
½ teaspoon garlic powder
2½ tablespoons chili powder
1 teaspoon dried oregano
¼ teaspoon ground red pepper
1 small bay leaf

Place beans in an airtight plastic bag; set aside.

Combine instant minced onion and next 3 ingredients; place in a small airtight plastic bag and, if desired, in a decorative paper bag, and label "Flavoring Packet."

Combine chili powder and remaining 3 ingredients; place in a small airtight plastic bag and, if desired, in a decorative paper bag, and label "Seasoning Packet."

Place 1 bag beans, 1 Flavoring Packet, and 1 Seasoning Packet in each gift container. **Yield:** 1 (3-bag) gift.

DIRECTIONS FOR GIFT CARD: Sort and wash beans; place in a large Dutch oven. Cover with water 2 inches above beans; let soak 8 hours. Drain.

Combine beans, Flavoring Packet, and 7 cups water in a large Dutch oven. Bring to a boil; cover, reduce heat, and simmer 1 hour, stirring occasionally.

Stir in 1 pound ground beef, cooked and drained, 1 (8-ounce) can tomato sauce, 1 (6-ounce) can tomato paste, and Seasoning Packet. Bring to a boil; reduce heat, and simmer, uncovered, 30 minutes, stirring occasionally. Remove and discard bay leaf. Yield: 11 cups.

NOTE: To use the quick-soak method, place beans in a Dutch oven; cover with water 2 inches above beans. Bring to a boil; boil 1 minute. Cover, remove from heat, and let stand 1 hour. Drain.

New Year's Day
Chili Mix

Bean-Pasta Soup Mix

If your thoughts drift to Christmas in July, act on the impulse and make a batch of this soup mix. It will keep for several months.

¾ cup dried onion flakes
½ cup dried parsley flakes
2 (½-ounce) jars dried celery flakes
3 tablespoons dried basil
3 tablespoons dried oregano
2 teaspoons garlic powder
2 teaspoons coarsely ground pepper
2 (2¼-ounce) jars beef-flavored bouillon
     granules
1 (16-ounce) package dried black-eyed peas
1 (16-ounce) package dried black beans
1 (16-ounce) package dried kidney beans
1 (16-ounce) package dried navy beans
1 (16-ounce) package small shell pasta

Combine first 7 ingredients; divide evenly into 6 portions, and place in 6 airtight plastic bags. Add 2 tablespoons plus ¼ teaspoon bouillon granules to each bag. Label "Herb Mix," and seal.

Combine black-eyed peas and next 3 ingredients. Divide evenly into 6 portions; place in 6 airtight plastic bags. Label "Bean Mix," and seal.

Place ⅓ cup pasta in 6 airtight plastic bags. Label "Pasta," and seal.

Place 1 Herb Mix, 1 Bean Mix, and 1 bag pasta in each gift container. **Yield:** 6 (3-bag) gifts.

DIRECTIONS FOR GIFT CARD: Sort and wash bean mix; place in a Dutch oven. Cover with water 2 inches above beans; let soak 8 hours. Drain.

Combine beans, 3 quarts water, herb mix, 1 carrot (scraped and chopped), and ⅔ cup chopped cooked ham in Dutch oven. Bring to a boil; reduce heat, and simmer 2½ hours, stirring occasionally.

Add 1 (14.5-ounce) can Mexican-style stewed tomatoes, undrained, and pasta; cook 20 minutes. Yield: 9 cups.

NOTE: To use the quick-soak method, place beans in a Dutch oven; cover with water 2 inches above beans. Bring to a boil; boil 1 minute. Cover, remove from heat, and let stand 1 hour. Drain.

Honeyed Peach Glaze (photo on page 134)

1 (12-ounce) jar peach preserves
⅓ cup honey
2 teaspoons prepared horseradish
½ teaspoon curry powder
½ teaspoon ground ginger

Combine all ingredients, stirring well. Spoon into an airtight container. Store in refrigerator up to 3 months. **Yield:** 1 cup.

DIRECTIONS FOR GIFT CARD: Store Honeyed Peach Glaze in refrigerator up to 3 months. Brush glaze over ham, pork, chicken, or Cornish hens during baking, or serve as an appetizer with cream cheese and crackers.

Pear Honey (photo on page 139)

3 large pears, peeled and quartered
    (1½ pounds)
4 cups sugar
1 (8-ounce) can crushed unsweetened
    pineapple, drained
1 tablespoon grated lemon rind
2 tablespoons fresh lemon juice

Position knife blade in food processor bowl; add pears. Process until finely chopped, stopping once to scrape down sides. (Do not puree.) Measure processed pear to equal 4 cups.

Combine 4 cups pear, sugar, and remaining ingredients in a heavy saucepan. Bring to a boil over medium heat; cook until sugar dissolves, stirring often. Reduce heat, and simmer 40 minutes or until mixture thickens, stirring often.

Spoon into hot, sterilized jars, filling to ¼ inch from top; wipe jar rims. Cover at once with metal lids, and screw on bands. Process in boiling-water bath 5 minutes. **Yield:** 3 half-pints.

DIRECTIONS FOR GIFT CARD: After opening, store Pear Honey in refrigerator. Let come to room temperature before serving.

Basil Jelly

1⅓ cups loosely packed fresh basil leaves
2 cups water
¾ cup white vinegar
¼ cup lemon juice
6 cups sugar
5 drops of green food coloring
1 (3-ounce) package liquid pectin

Combine first 4 ingredients in a saucepan; bring to a boil. Cover, remove from heat, and let stand 10 minutes.

Pour vinegar mixture through a wire mesh strainer into a Dutch oven, discarding basil leaves. Add sugar and food coloring, and bring to a boil, stirring constantly. Stir in pectin; boil 1 minute. Remove from heat, and skim off foam with a metal spoon.

Pour jelly into hot, sterilized jars, filling to ¼ inch from top; wipe jar rims. Cover at once with metal lids, and screw on bands. Process in boiling-water bath 5 minutes. **Yield:** 6 half-pints.

Orange-Grapefruit Jelly

6½ cups sugar
2 cups water
¼ cup plus 2 tablespoons lemon juice
1 (6-ounce) can frozen orange juice
    concentrate, thawed and undiluted
1 (6-ounce) can frozen grapefruit juice
    concentrate, thawed and undiluted
1 (6-ounce) package liquid pectin

Combine sugar and water in a large Dutch oven; bring to a rolling boil. Add lemon juice, and boil 1 minute. Stir in juice concentrates and pectin; return to a rolling boil, and boil 1 minute, stirring constantly. Remove from heat, and skim off foam with a metal spoon.

Pour into hot, sterilized jars, filling to ¼ inch from top; wipe jar rims. Cover at once with metal lids, and screw on bands. Process in boiling-water bath 5 minutes. **Yield:** 9 half-pints.

Jeweled
Pepper
Chutney

To The Marvins
From The Byars

Jeweled Pepper Chutney

Glistening jewels of red bell pepper adorn cheese and crackers. Package jars of chutney along with cheese and crackers in an unexpected container like a small galvanized bucket.

8 large red bell peppers, cut into
       ¼-inch cubes
4 jalapeño peppers, finely chopped
8 cloves garlic, minced
2½ cups cider vinegar (5% acidity)
2 cups firmly packed brown sugar
2 cups sugar
2 cups golden raisins
⅓ cup finely chopped crystallized
       ginger (2 ounces)

Combine all ingredients in a large Dutch oven, and bring to a boil. Reduce heat, and simmer, uncovered, 1 hour and 45 minutes, stirring occasionally.

Spoon into hot, sterilized jars, filling to ½ inch from top. Remove air bubbles, and wipe jar rims. Cover at once with metal lids, and screw on bands. Process in boiling-water bath 10 minutes. **Yield:** 6 half-pints.

DIRECTIONS FOR GIFT CARD: After opening, store Jeweled Pepper Chutney in refrigerator. Serve with cheese and crackers.

Peanut-Butterscotch Sauce

This buttery-rich peanut sauce is meant to be served warm and gooey over a scoop or two of the best vanilla ice cream.

1½ cups firmly packed brown sugar
⅔ cup light corn syrup
¼ cup butter or margarine
1 (5-ounce) can evaporated milk
½ cup coarsely chopped dry roasted peanuts
¼ cup creamy peanut butter
⅛ teaspoon salt

Combine first 3 ingredients in a heavy saucepan. Cook over medium heat, stirring constantly, until mixture reaches soft ball stage or candy thermometer registers 234°. Remove from heat; stir in milk and remaining ingredients. Store in an airtight container in refrigerator. **Yield:** 2½ cups.

DIRECTIONS FOR GIFT CARD: Store Peanut-Butterscotch Sauce in an airtight container in refrigerator. Reheat sauce, and serve warm over vanilla ice cream.

Hot Pineapple Sauce

1 (12-ounce) jar apricot preserves
1 (8-ounce) can unsweetened crushed
       pineapple, drained
½ cup finely chopped sweet red pepper
¼ cup finely chopped green onions
2 tablespoons finely chopped jalapeño
       peppers
2 tablespoons balsamic or red wine
       vinegar

Combine all ingredients in a small saucepan; bring to a boil, stirring often. Reduce heat, and simmer 5 minutes. Spoon sauce into a gift container; cover and chill. **Yield:** 1⅓ cups.

DIRECTIONS FOR GIFT CARD: Heat Hot Pineapple Sauce in a small saucepan; serve with pork, ham, and turkey.

Barbecue Sauce

1 (32-ounce) bottle ketchup
1 (12-ounce) bottle chili sauce
1 (12-ounce) can beer
1¾ cups firmly packed brown sugar
1½ cups white vinegar
1 cup lemon juice
½ cup steak sauce
⅓ cup prepared mustard
¼ cup Worcestershire sauce
2 tablespoons pepper
1 tablespoon dry mustard
2 tablespoons vegetable oil
1 tablespoon soy sauce

Combine all ingredients in a Dutch oven; cook over medium heat 8 minutes, stirring occasionally. Pour into bottles; chill up to 3 months. **Yield:** 2½ quarts.

DIRECTIONS FOR GIFT CARD: Store Barbecue Sauce in refrigerator up to 3 months. Use as a basting sauce for pork or chicken during cooking.

Stir-Fry Sauce

1 (15-ounce) bottle soy sauce
1½ cups Chablis or other dry white wine
½ cup dry sherry
⅓ cup firmly packed brown sugar
2 cloves garlic, halved
2 tablespoons chicken-flavored bouillon granules
2 tablespoons grated fresh gingerroot
2 teaspoons black peppercorns
1½ teaspoons sesame oil

Combine all ingredients; cover and chill 8 hours. Pour through a large wire-mesh strainer into bottles, discarding solids. Store in refrigerator up to 4 weeks. **Yield:** 4½ cups.

DIRECTIONS FOR GIFT CARD: Store Stir-Fry Sauce in refrigerator up to 4 weeks.

To use, marinate 1 pound chicken or pork strips in ½ cup Stir-Fry Sauce 30 minutes. Drain, reserving sauce. Bring sauce to a boil; set aside.

Cook meat in 1 tablespoon vegetable oil in a large skillet, stirring constantly, until done; remove from skillet, and drain on paper towels.

Add 4 cups mixed vegetables to skillet; stir-fry 2 minutes or until crisp-tender. Combine 1 tablespoon cornstarch, ½ cup water, and reserved sauce; add to vegetable mixture. Cook 1 minute. Add meat, and cook until thoroughly heated. Serve over rice. Yield: 4 servings.

Raspberry Vinegar

Choose clear decorative bottles to allow the crimson color of the Raspberry Vinegar to shine through.

2 cups fresh raspberries
2 (17-ounce) bottles white wine vinegar
2 (3-inch) sticks cinnamon
½ cup honey

Combine raspberries and vinegar in a nonmetal bowl; cover and let stand at room temperature 8 hours.

Transfer to a large nonaluminum saucepan, and add cinnamon; bring to a boil. Reduce heat, and simmer, uncovered, 3 minutes. Remove from heat; stir in honey, and cool.

Pour through a large wire-mesh strainer into bottles or jars, discarding solids. Seal with a cork or an airtight lid. Store vinegar at room temperature 2 weeks before using. **Yield:** 4 cups.

NOTE: You can substitute 1 (16-ounce) package frozen whole raspberries, thawed and drained, for the fresh raspberries. Yield: 3½ cups.

DIRECTIONS FOR GIFT CARD: Store at room temperature 2 weeks before using. Use in vinaigrettes or marinades.

Rasberry Vinegar

Stir-fry Sauce

30 min
Stir-

Pickled Vegetables

Pickled Vegetables

A harvest of colorful vegetables stars in this spirited meal accompaniment. Cover the jar lids with squares of handmade paper, and tie with a gold ribbon.

1 large head cauliflower
8 cups water
4 cups white vinegar (5% acidity)
¾ cup honey
3 tablespoons mustard seeds
1½ teaspoons celery seeds
½ teaspoon black peppercorns
1 pound trimmed, peeled baby carrots
6 stalks celery, cut into thin 2-inch strips
1 medium-size green bell pepper, cut into
      thin 1½-inch strips
1 medium-size red bell pepper, cut into thin
      1½-inch strips
1 (16-ounce) can whole green beans, drained
8 small cloves garlic
8 small serrano chiles
1 teaspoon salt

   Remove large outer leaves of cauliflower; break into flowerets. Set aside.
   Combine water and next 5 ingredients in a nonaluminum Dutch oven. Bring to a boil; reduce heat, and simmer, uncovered, 30 minutes. Skim off foam with a metal spoon. Add carrots. Bring to a boil; reduce heat, and simmer 3 minutes. Add cauliflower and celery. Bring to a boil; reduce heat, and simmer 5 minutes. Add pepper strips and green beans, and simmer 3 minutes.
   Spoon vegetables evenly into 8 (2-cup) hot, sterilized jars. Pour hot vinegar mixture over vegetables, evenly distributing spices. Add 1 clove garlic, 1 serrano chile, and ⅛ teaspoon salt to each jar. Cool.
   Seal jars. Chill one week before serving. **Yield:** 8 (2-cup) gifts.

DIRECTIONS FOR GIFT CARD: Store Pickled Vegetables in refrigerator up to 3 weeks.

Brandied Cheese Spread

Toasted slivers of almonds plus a hint of coffee and brandy show off this sweet cheese spread to its best advantage. Slices of fresh fruit and crisp gingersnaps provide fitting companionship.

¼ teaspoon instant coffee granules
1 tablespoon hot water
1 (8-ounce) package cream cheese, softened
¼ cup sugar
2 tablespoons sour cream
2 tablespoons brandy
1 (2-ounce) package slivered almonds,
      toasted and chopped

   Dissolve coffee granules in water in a large mixing bowl. Add cream cheese and next 3 ingredients; beat at medium speed of an electric mixer until blended. Stir in almonds.
   Spoon mixture into an airtight container, and chill up to 1 week. **Yield:** 1½ cups.

DIRECTIONS FOR GIFT CARD: Store Brandied Cheese Spread in refrigerator up to 1 week. Serve with gingersnaps or sliced apples and pears.

Boursin Cheese Spread

White and smooth with a buttery texture, this garlicky cheese spread is flecked with an assortment of herbs. For gift giving, stow the spread in a crock, and then add it to a colorful gift bag filled with fresh fruit, a crusty loaf of French bread, and wine.

4 (8-ounce) packages cream cheese, softened
1 (8-ounce) carton whipped butter
2 cloves garlic, pressed
½ teaspoon dried oregano
¼ teaspoon dried basil
¼ teaspoon dried marjoram
¼ teaspoon dried thyme
¼ teaspoon pepper

Beat cream cheese in a medium mixing bowl at medium speed of an electric mixer until creamy; add butter and remaining ingredients, beating until blended. Spoon into airtight containers. Store in refrigerator up to 1 week. **Yield:** 3½ cups.

DIRECTIONS FOR GIFT CARD: Store Boursin Cheese Spread in refrigerator up to 1 week. Serve with French bread or crackers.

Spicy Cheese Spread with Pita Chips

1 (8-ounce) package cream cheese, softened
1 tablespoon milk
1 clove garlic, crushed
½ teaspoon dried oregano
½ teaspoon chili powder
⅛ teaspoon ground cumin
Paprika
Pita Chips

Combine first 6 ingredients in a small bowl, stirring until blended. Spoon into an airtight container, and sprinkle with paprika. Cover and chill at least 8 hours. Serve with Pita Chips. **Yield:** 1 cup.

Pita Chips

4 large pita bread rounds
⅓ cup butter or margarine, melted
⅛ teaspoon dried oregano
⅛ teaspoon chili powder
⅛ teaspoon ground red pepper

Separate each bread round into 2 pieces; cut each piece into 8 wedges. Place in a large heavy-duty, zip-top plastic bag.

Combine butter and remaining 3 ingredients; drizzle over wedges. Seal bag, and shake gently to coat wedges.

Place on ungreased baking sheets. Bake at 300° for 30 minutes or until crisp and lightly browned. Cool. Store in an airtight container. **Yield:** 64 chips.

DIRECTIONS FOR GIFT CARD: Store Spicy Cheese Spread in refrigerator up to 1 week. Serve with Pita Chips.

Herb and Pepper Cheese Spread

(photo on page 135)

2 (8-ounce) packages cream cheese, softened
½ cup butter or margarine, softened
2 teaspoons chopped fresh chives
1 teaspoon dried basil
1 teaspoon caraway seeds
1 teaspoon dillseeds
⅓ cup finely chopped red, green, or yellow
   bell pepper

Combine all ingredients except bell pepper in a large mixing bowl; beat at medium speed of an electric mixer until smooth. Stir in bell pepper.

Spoon cheese spread into crocks or airtight containers. Store in refrigerator up to 1 week. **Yield:** 2¾ cups.

DIRECTIONS FOR GIFT CARD: Store Herb and Pepper Cheese Spread in refrigerator up to 1 week. Serve with bagel chips or crackers.

Chocolate-Almond Spread

2 cups (12 ounces) semisweet chocolate
    morsels
⅓ cup light corn syrup
⅓ cup whipping cream
½ cup chopped almonds, toasted
1 teaspoon almond extract

Combine first 3 ingredients in top of a double boiler; bring water to a boil. Reduce heat to low, and cook until chocolate melts, stirring occasionally. Remove from heat; stir in almonds and almond extract.

Spoon evenly into 2 (1-cup) gift containers. Store in refrigerator up to 1 month. **Yield:** about 2 cups.

DIRECTIONS FOR GIFT CARD: Store Chocolate-Almond Spread in refrigerator up to 1 month. Serve with cookies, croissants, or fruit.

Chocolate-Almond Spread

Cashew-Honey Butter

Roasted cashews are processed until smooth and spreadable, then sweetly kissed with honey for a blissful butter.

1   cup dry roasted cashews
2   tablespoons vegetable oil
1   tablespoon honey

Place cashews in container of an electric blender; process at low speed until finely chopped, stopping once to scrape down sides.

Add oil and honey; process at high speed until smooth, stopping once to scrape down sides. Serve on crackers or bread. Store in refrigerator up to 1 month. **Yield:** ¾ cup.

DIRECTIONS FOR GIFT CARD: Store Cashew-Honey Butter in refrigerator up to 1 month. Serve with crackers or bagels.

Hot Creole Seasoning Mix

½   cup salt
⅓   cup paprika
¼   cup ground white pepper
¼   cup garlic powder
¼   cup onion powder
3   tablespoons ground red pepper
2   tablespoons dried oregano
2   tablespoons dried thyme
1   tablespoon black pepper
1   teaspoon ground bay leaves

Combine all ingredients in a jar; cover and shake mixture until well blended. Store in an airtight container. **Yield:** 2 cups.

DIRECTIONS FOR GIFT CARD: Use seasoning mix in gumbo or jambalaya.

Jerk Seasoning Rub

Barbecue Jamaican style with this spicy mixture. For the most intense flavor, use freshly ground spices in the rub.

1½   tablespoons sugar
1   tablespoon onion powder
1   tablespoon dried thyme
2   teaspoons ground allspice
2   teaspoons freshly ground black pepper
2   teaspoons ground red pepper
1   teaspoon salt
¾   teaspoon ground nutmeg
¼   teaspoon ground cloves

Combine all ingredients; store in an airtight container. **Yield:** ⅓ cup.

DIRECTIONS FOR GIFT CARD: Rub or sprinkle Jerk Seasoning Rub on chicken or seafood before broiling or grilling.

Southwestern Spice Rub

1   tablespoon cumin seeds
1   teaspoon coriander seeds
8   dried chiles, stemmed and seeded
1   tablespoon brown sugar
1   teaspoon ground cinnamon
½   teaspoon garlic powder
½   teaspoon salt
¼   teaspoon black pepper
¼   teaspoon ground red pepper

Cook cumin and coriander seeds in a small skillet over low heat, stirring constantly, 3 minutes. Combine seeds, chiles, and remaining ingredients in an electric blender; process until mixture resembles coarse powder. Store in an airtight container. **Yield:** ⅔ cup.

DIRECTIONS FOR GIFT CARD: Sprinkle Southwestern Spice Rub on chicken, beef, and pork before grilling, broiling, or baking.

Mustard-Garlic Marinade

½ cup white vinegar
¼ cup dry mustard
¼ cup olive oil
2 tablespoons crushed garlic
½ teaspoon salt
½ teaspoon dried tarragon
¼ teaspoon freshly ground pepper
Dash of ground red pepper

Combine all ingredients in a small bowl; whisk until smooth and blended. Pour mixture into a bottle. Store in refrigerator up to 1 month. **Yield:** 1 cup.

DIRECTIONS FOR GIFT CARD: Store Mustard-Garlic Marinade in refrigerator up to 1 month. Use as a marinade for fish or pork tenderloin.

Herbed Mayonnaise

Parsley, chives, and cilantro spike this simple-to-prepare mayonnaise with straightforward herb flavor. A touch of grated lime rind adds balance to the blend.

1 cup mayonnaise
2 tablespoons chopped fresh parsley
2 teaspoons freeze-dried chives
2 teaspoons dried cilantro
1 teaspoon grated lime rind

Combine all ingredients; spoon into an airtight container. Store in refrigerator up to 2 months. **Yield:** 1 cup.

DIRECTIONS FOR GIFT CARD: Store Herbed Mayonnaise in refrigerator up to 2 months.

Ginger Dressing

⅓ cup vegetable oil
⅓ cup reduced-sodium soy sauce
⅓ cup white vinegar
1 teaspoon ground ginger
1 teaspoon garlic powder
Dash of pepper

Combine all ingredients in a jar. Cover tightly, and shake vigorously. Pour into a bottle. Store in refrigerator up to 1 month. **Yield:** about 1 cup.

DIRECTIONS FOR GIFT CARD: Store Ginger Dressing in refrigerator up to 1 month. Serve as a salad dressing or use as a marinade for pork.

Poppy Seed Dressing

1 (6-ounce) can frozen limeade, thawed and undiluted
½ cup honey
¼ teaspoon salt
¾ cup vegetable oil
2 teaspoons poppy seeds

Combine first 3 ingredients in container of an electric blender; process 20 seconds. With blender on high, gradually add oil in a slow, steady stream. Stir in poppy seeds. Pour mixture into a bottle. Store in refrigerator up to 1 month. **Yield:** 2 cups.

DIRECTIONS FOR GIFT CARD: Store Poppy Seed Dressing in refrigerator up to 1 month. Serve over fruit salad.

Index

Metric Equivalents

The recipes that appear in this cookbook use the standard United States method for measuring liquid and dry or solid ingredients (teaspoons, tablespoons, and cups). The information in the following charts is provided to help cooks outside the U.S. successfully use these recipes. All equivalents are approximate.

Metric Equivalents for Different Types of Ingredients

A standard cup measure of a dry or solid ingredient will vary in weight depending on the type of ingredient. A standard cup of liquid is the same volume for any type of liquid. Use the following chart when converting standard cup measures to grams (weight) or milliliters (volume).

Standard Cup	Fine Powder (ex. flour)	Grain (ex. rice)	Granular (ex. sugar)	Liquid Solids (ex. butter)	Liquid (ex. milk)
1	140 g	150 g	190 g	200 g	240 ml
¾	105 g	113 g	143 g	150 g	180 ml
⅔	93 g	100 g	125 g	133 g	160 ml
½	70 g	75 g	95 g	100 g	120 ml
⅓	47 g	50 g	63 g	67 g	80 ml
¼	35 g	38 g	48 g	50 g	60 ml
⅛	18 g	19 g	24 g	25 g	30 ml

Metric Equivalents for Liquid Ingredients by Volume

¼ tsp				=	1 ml
½ tsp				=	2 ml
1 tsp				=	5 ml
3 tsp	= 1 tbls		= ½ fl oz	=	15 ml
	2 tbls	= ⅛ cup	= 1 fl oz	=	30 ml
	4 tbls	= ¼ cup	= 2 fl oz	=	60 ml
	5⅓ tbls	= ⅓ cup	= 3 fl oz	=	80 ml
	8 tbls	= ½ cup	= 4 fl oz	=	120 ml
	10⅔ tbls	= ⅔ cup	= 5 fl oz	=	160 ml
	12 tbls	= ¾ cup	= 6 fl oz	=	180 ml
	16 tbls	= 1 cup	= 8 fl oz	=	240 ml
1 pt	= 2 cups	= 16 fl oz	=	480 ml	
1 qt	= 4 cups	= 32 fl oz	=	960 ml	
		33 fl oz	= 1000 ml	= 1 l	

Useful Equivalents for Dry Ingredients by Weight

(To convert ounces to grams, multiply the number of ounces by 30.)

1 oz	=	¹⁄₁₆ lb	=	30 g
4 oz	=	¼ lb	=	120 g
8 oz	=	½ lb	=	240 g
12 oz	=	¾ lb	=	360 g
16 oz	=	1 lb	=	480 g

Useful Equivalents for Length

(To convert inches to centimeters, multiply the number of inches by 2.5.)

1 in	=		= 2.5 cm	
6 in	= ½ ft		= 15 cm	
12 in	= 1 ft		= 30 cm	
36 in	= 3 ft	= 1 yd	= 90 cm	
40 in	=		= 100 cm	= 1 m

Useful Equivalents for Cooking/Oven Temperatures

	Fahrenheit	Celcius	Gas Mark
Freeze Water	32° F	0° C	
Room Temperature	68° F	20° C	
Boil Water	212° F	100° C	
Bake	325° F	160° C	3
	350° F	180° C	4
	375° F	190° C	5
	400° F	200° C	6
	425° F	220° C	7
	450° F	230° C	8
Broil			Grill